1st EDITION

Perspectives on Modern World History

Prohibition

1st EDITION

Perspectives on Modern World History

Prohibition

Sylvia Engdahl

Editor

GREENHAVEN PRESS
A part of Gale, Cengage Learning

 GALE
CENGAGE Learning·

Detroit • New York • San Francisco • New Haven, Conn • Waterville, Maine • London

GALE
CENGAGE Learning·

Elizabeth Des Chenes, *Director, Publishing Solutions*

© 2013 Greenhaven Press, a part of Gale, Cengage Learning.

Gale and Greenhaven Press are registered trademarks used herein under license.

For more information, contact:
Greenhaven Press
27500 Drake Rd.
Farmington Hills, MI 48331-3535
Or you can visit our Internet site at gale.cengage.com.

For product information and technology assistance, contact us at
Gale Customer Support, 1-800-877-4253.

For permission to use material from this text or product, submit all requests online at
www.cengage.com/permissions.

Further permissions questions can be e-mailed to permissionrequest@cengage.com.

Articles in Greenhaven Press anthologies are often edited for length to meet page requirements. In addition, original titles of these works are changed to clearly present the main thesis and to explicitly indicate the author's opinion. Every effort is made to ensure that Greenhaven Press accurately reflects the original intent of the authors. Every effort has been made to trace the owners of copyrighted material.

Cover images © Everett Collection/Alamy and © Bettmann/Corbis.

LIBRARY OF CONGRESS CATALOGING-IN-PUBLICATION DATA

Prohibition / Sylvia Engdahl, book editor.
   p. cm. -- (Perspectives on modern world history)
   Includes bibliographical references and index.
   ISBN 978-0-7377-6370-6 (hbk.)
  1. Prohibition--United States--History. 2. Temperance--United States--History. I. Engdahl, Sylvia.
  HV5089.P746 2012
  363.4'10973--dc23   2012028206

Printed in the United States of America
1 2 3 4 5 6 7 16 15 14 13 12

CONTENTS

he says; the states should be given a chance to vote on a constitutional amendment to permanently banish the saloon business.

smuggling—both across the Canadian border and by sea. Rumrunner ships were intercepted by the Coast Guard.

legalized liquor business is the leading cause of human misery, and it is a parasite that saps the vitality of the nation. Though it is condemned by reason, science, social reform, and morality, the liquor industry has continued to thrive, and the major political parties have ignored the problem. He appeals to voters to rise up and banish the industry without compromise.

CHAPTER 3   Personal Narratives

FOREWORD

"History cannot give us a program for the future, but it can give us a fuller understanding of ourselves, and of our common humanity, so that we can better face the future."

—Robert Penn Warren,
American poet and novelist

The history of each nation is punctuated by momentous events that represent turning points for that nation, with an impact felt far beyond its borders. These events—displaying the full range of human capabilities, from violence, greed, and ignorance to heroism, courage, and strength—are nearly always complicated and multifaceted. Any student of history faces the challenge of grasping the many strands that constitute such world-changing events as wars, social movements, and environmental disasters. But understanding these significant historic events can be enhanced by exposure to a variety of perspectives, whether of people involved intimately or of ones observing from a distance of miles or years. Understanding can also be increased by learning about the controversies surrounding such events and exploring hot-button issues from multiple angles. Finally, true understanding of important historic events involves knowledge of the events' human impact—of the ways such events affected people in their everyday lives—all over the world.

Perspectives on Modern World History examines global historic events from the twentieth century onward by presenting analysis and observation from numerous vantage points. Each volume offers high school, early college level, and general interest readers a thematically arranged anthology of previously published materials that address a major historical event, with an emphasis on international coverage. Each volume opens with background information on the event, then presents the controversies surrounding that event, and concludes with first-person narratives from people who lived through the event or were affected by it. By providing primary sources from the time of the event, as well as relevant commentary surrounding the event, this series can be used to inform debate, help develop critical thinking skills, increase global awareness, and enhance an understanding of international perspectives on history.

Material in each volume is selected from a diverse range of sources, including journals, magazines, newspapers, nonfiction books, personal narratives, speeches, congressional testimony, government documents, pamphlets, organization newsletters, and position papers. Articles taken from these sources are carefully edited and introduced to provide context and background. Each volume of Perspectives on Modern World History includes an array of views on events of global significance. Much of the material comes from international sources and from US sources that provide extensive international coverage.

Each volume in the Perspectives on Modern World History series also includes:

- A full-color **world map**, offering context and geographic perspective.
- An annotated **table of contents** that provides a brief summary of each essay in the volume.
- An **introduction** specific to the volume topic.
- For each viewpoint, a brief **introduction** that has notes about the author and source of the viewpoint, and that provides a summary of its main points.
- Full-color **charts**, **graphs**, **maps**, and other visual representations.

- Informational **sidebars** that explore the lives of key individuals, give background on historical events, or explain scientific or technical concepts.
- A **glossary** that defines key terms, as needed.
- A **chronology** of important dates preceding, during, and immediately following the event.
- A **bibliography** of additional books, periodicals, and websites for further research.
- A comprehensive **subject index** that offers access to people, places, and events cited in the text.

Perspectives on Modern World History is designed for a broad spectrum of readers who want to learn more about not only history but also current events, political science, government, international relations, and sociology—students doing research for class assignments or debates, teachers and faculty seeking to supplement course materials, and others wanting to improve their understanding of history. Each volume of Perspectives on Modern World History is designed to illuminate a complicated event, to spark debate, and to show the human perspective behind the world's most significant happenings of recent decades.

INTRODUCTION

For a short period in the early twentieth century—just under fourteen years—the manufacture and sale of alcoholic beverages was illegal in the United States. This period is known as the Prohibition era. Despite its brevity, Prohibition had far-reaching effects on US society and on the relationship between Americans and the federal government—effects that involved much more than the issue of whether or not people should be allowed to drink liquor. Those effects are still being felt today.

The prohibition of alcohol was not a sudden event. Throughout the nineteenth century, and especially during its second half, there had been a growing temperance movement. Temperance originally meant moderation in the use of alcohol, but in the eyes of most supporters it eventually came to mean abolishing it entirely. Many churches exhorted people not to drink, but preaching against the evils of alcohol was not confined to churches. Emotional books and speeches on the subject were common. Schools taught that alcohol itself, not merely the abuse of it, was harmful. One by one, states passed prohibition laws of their own. The first to do so was Maine in 1851, and by the time national Prohibition went into effect in 1920, thirty-three states, covering 63 percent of the US population, were already "dry."

One reason for the strong opposition to alcohol was its association with saloons. The saloons that existed before Prohibition were disreputable places. Middle-class men did not patronize them. Respectable women never entered them, except occasionally as crusaders agitating for their destruction. Working-class men who visited them were all too likely to spend long hours there, get drunk, and subsequently neglect or abuse their families;

anti-alcohol publicity often featured the starving children of fathers who spent their wages on drink. Moreover, saloons were centers of gambling, prostitution, and gathering places for crooked officials and police who were bribed to disregard violations of local laws. It was commonly thought that eliminating saloons would bring about a dramatic reduction in crime. The Anti-Saloon League, founded in 1893, became the most powerful of the organizations that lobbied for Prohibition, and it gained widespread support.

Another factor that led to national Prohibition was the United States' entry into World War I. Many people believed that drinking was immoral and thus incompatible with the high ideals that underlay public support for the "War to End All Wars." The sale of liquor to soldiers was forbidden, and eventually the use of grain to manufacture alcoholic beverages was banned as a wartime measure to reserve cereal grains for food for the troops. The public, dedicated to the war effort, was in a mood to make sacrifices. Furthermore, many beer brewers were of German descent, and agitators against breweries exploited the strong anti-German sentiment that existed during the war years.

All these factors combined to create a public demand for Prohibition to become nationwide and permanent. But Congress did not have the authority to pass a national prohibition law because making laws that controlled what individual citizens could do—as opposed to what government could do—was not among the powers authorized by the US Constitution. Today, ways around this restriction have been developed—many things, such as illegal drugs, are forbidden through the federal government's power to control interstate commerce. But at the time that Prohibition was proposed, most legal experts believed that alcohol could be banned only by a constitutional amendment. Such an amendment was first considered by Congress in 1914, but failed to receive the two-thirds majority vote needed for it to pass. When it was introduced again, in 1917, it did pass and was submitted to the states for ratification. It became the Eighteenth Amendment when ratified in 1919, and went into effect one year later, on January 16, 1920.

The result was not what people had expected. As journalist Herbert Asbury wrote in his 1950 book *The Great Illusion*:

> For more than a hundred years they had been indoctrinated with the idea that the destruction of the liquor traffic was the will of God and would provide the answers to most, if not all, of mankind's problems. . . . They had expected to be greeted, when the great day came, by a covey of angels bearing gifts of peace, happiness, prosperity, and salvation, which they had been assured would be theirs when the rum demon had been scotched. Instead they were met by a horde of bootleggers, moonshiners, rumrunners, hijackers, gangsters, racketeers, trigger men, venal judges, corrupt police, crooked politicians, and speakeasy operators, all bearing the twin symbols of the Eighteenth Amendment—the tommy gun and the poisoned cup.

Supporters of Prohibition believed that it would be relatively easy to enforce. They did not foresee the reaction of the public to federal restrictions on private conduct. Adoption of such restrictions on a national scale was an extremely radical step—a 1926 editorial in the *New Republic* called it "the most radical political and social experiment of our day"—and many citizens, even those who had not previously been heavy drinkers, resented it. Laws affecting individuals had in the past been made only at the local and state level—even the income tax, which had not been introduced until 1913, was imposed only on the wealthy. By now, the US public is used to the idea of ordinary people's actions being regulated by federal laws. It was Prohibition that brought about this change in outlook. Unfortunately, it also brought about a lasting attitude of disrespect for the law in general.

It might be thought that because so many states already had prohibition laws, the majority of the population would not have cared. But the dry states were predominantly rural, agricultural ones. The attitude in big cities, especially those containing large numbers of immigrants from countries where moderate drinking was an integral part of the culture, was quite different. Also, people who wanted liquor in dry states could no longer have it shipped to them, a practice that under many state laws—those intended merely to abolish saloons—had been legal. So the market for bootleg liquor was large, and it led to the rise of organized crime, a new phenomenon that arose to meet the demand and has continued to thrive ever since.

Notorious gangsters such as Al Capone gained wealth and power beyond anything previously imagined, and by many they were viewed as celebrities. Violence as well as illegal trafficking became rampant. Shoot-outs—between rival gangs, between federal agents and gangsters, and between the Coast Guard and rumrunners—became common. Police and federal law enforcement officers made little headway in stemming the liquor traffic, and a good many of them were corrupted by bribes. The federal courts were overwhelmed; a 1931 government document observed: "The effect of the huge volume of liquor prosecutions, which has come to these courts under prohibition, has injured their dignity, impaired their efficiency, and endangered the wholesome respect for them which once obtained. Instead of being impressive tribunals of superior jurisdiction, they have had to do the work of police courts."

Lack of respect for courts and for corrupt officials, however, was minor compared to the prevailing lack of respect for the prohibition law itself. Previously, most people had considered themselves law-abiding citizens.

Now flouting the law became socially acceptable. This was partly due to the obvious hypocrisy of numerous government officials, such as President Warren G. Harding, who were known to drink bootleg liquor behind closed doors. But it was mainly the result of the excitement and glamour attached to forbidden drinking. People who had once drunk only wine with meals now went to speakeasies (illegal bars that required a password for admittance) and drank cocktails. It was estimated that there were more than a hundred thousand speakeasies in New York alone. The speakeasies, unlike the old saloons, were patronized by women as well as men. Few middle-class women had drunk hard liquor before; under Prohibition doing so became fashionable.

Contrary to common belief, the Eighteenth Amendment did not prohibit possession or consumption of liquor, although some state laws did. Only the manufacture, sale, and transportation of alcohol were banned under federal law. The National Prohibition Act, known as the Volstead Act, specifically stated that it was legal to drink in private homes (any liquor found elsewhere was presumed to be for sale) and to offer drinks to bona fide guests. Thus people who could afford to do so stocked up before the effective date of the amendment, and were able to smuggle bootleg liquor into their homes later. But the poor, who were accustomed to drinking beer, were unable get it. Bootleggers did not deal in beer, because distilled liquor was easier to produce and transport and, because of its higher alcohol content, was far more profitable. Many people therefore came to feel that the Volstead Act discriminated against the poor. Most supporters of the Eighteenth Amendment had not expected beer and wine to be covered by the law; they were stunned when Congress set the maximum amount of alcohol allowed in a beverage at a mere one-half of 1 percent. Although after the first few months it became legal to make "fruit juices"—i.e., cider and wine—in the home for private consumption, this was not practical for most people and did little to help the situation caused by what many considered an overzealous use of the power given to Congress.

With the dramatic rise in crime during the Prohibition era came a need for stronger measures than had previously been considered acceptable. Enforcement officials, desperate for a way to cope with the ever-increasing liquor traffic, turned to methods that many people believed were unconstitutional under the Fourth and Fifth Amendments. The Supreme Court, too, believed enforcement of Prohibition had top priority. Thus it upheld first the search of automobiles without a warrant, and then the use of wiretapping by government agents—practices originally adopted to catch bootleggers that have become routine today in combating drug dealers and terrorists. The crisis provoked by Prohibition weakened Americans' reluctance to allow such measures. Whether the impact of Prohibition on the rights of innocent citizens can be justified is still debated today.

In the late 1920s, when it became apparent that Prohibition was not working and creating worse problems than those it was intended to solve, a movement toward repeal of the Eighteenth Amendment began to grow. But the majority of citizens still supported the amendment, at least publicly. Some blamed the problems on liquor itself rather than on what people were doing to obtain it, and held to the belief that the desire to drink could eventually be stamped out. Others simply thought that abstention from alcohol was a moral issue and that the government ought to stand firm for morality. Residents of agricultural states, who had not come into personal contact with the crime that flourished in the cities and along the Canadian border, did not perceive the law as harmful. And dedicated members of the Anti-Saloon League did not want to admit defeat.

At the close of 1927, the Association Against the Prohibition Amendment (AAPA), which had been dormant since the amendment's ratification, decided to launch a campaign for repeal. In 1929 it was joined by the newly formed Women's Organization for National Prohibition Reform (WONPR), which emphasized the dangers that prohibition-related crime posed to children. These two organizations were instrumental in raising support for repeal. Yet as late as 1931, the Wickersham Commission Report on Alcohol Prohibition, which stated in detail how Prohibition was failing, recommended that it be retained.

Another issue arose during the Great Depression. Before the Eighteenth Amendment's adoption, the government had derived a large percentage of its revenue from liquor taxes. With times hard and funds scarce, that revenue was needed again. People who favored Prohibition in principle began to feel that it was costing the government too much money. Then, in July 1932, the immensely popular Franklin D. Roosevelt, to whom many people looked for help in ending the Depression, advocated repeal in his speech accepting the Democratic Party's presidential nomination. That turned the tide. Repeal was a feature of his campaign platform and became a significant factor in the Democrats' rise to power. Shortly after President Roosevelt took office, Congress passed a bill legalizing beer and wine. The Twenty-first Amendment, which repealed the Eighteenth, soon followed. The bill creating it was passed by Congress only six days after its introduction.

"It was as if someone were opening a bottle of champagne," wrote historian David Kyvig in *Repealing Prohibition*. "At first the cork moved slowly and only under great pressure. But once it reached a certain point, the cork literally exploded out of the neck. The final stage in the complicated process, state approval [ratification] of a new amendment, was completed more quickly than in any previous constitutional change in the nation's history." On December 5, 1933, Roosevelt issued a presidential proclamation announcing the end of national Prohibition, and what had once been called the "noble experiment" passed into history.

Today, some historians say that Prohibition succeeded because liquor consumption fell. But this assessment depends on what is meant by "succeeded." As *Reason* magazine editor Radley Balko writes on his blog:

> To call alcohol prohibition a "success," one would have to consider overall consumption of alcohol in America the *only* relevant criteria. You'd have to ignore the precipitous rise in homicides and other violent crime; the rise in hospitalizations due to alcohol poisoning; the number of people blinded or killed by drinking toxic, black market gin; the corrupting influence on government officials, from beat cops to the halls of Congress to [President Warren G.] Harding's attorney general; and the erosion of the rule of law.

Defenders mention that there was a significant drop in deaths from cirrhosis of the liver, a disease caused by alcoholism. In reply, critics point out that this drop was offset by the blindness, paralysis, and death suffered by thousands of victims who drank denatured industrial alcohol, either intentionally or unknowingly when bootleggers mixed it with liquor to stretch the supply.

The majority of Americans, both at the time the Twenty-first Amendment was adopted and since, have believed that the attempt to ban alcoholic beverages was a tragic failure, and that it demonstrated the impossibility of trying to change human nature by government decree. Many also consider it responsible for the subsequent pushing of drugs by the crime syndicates it created. The question of whether its long-term effects have harmed the nation is a controversial one. *Perspectives on Modern World History: Prohibition* examines the Prohibition era in the United States and its impact on the nation today.

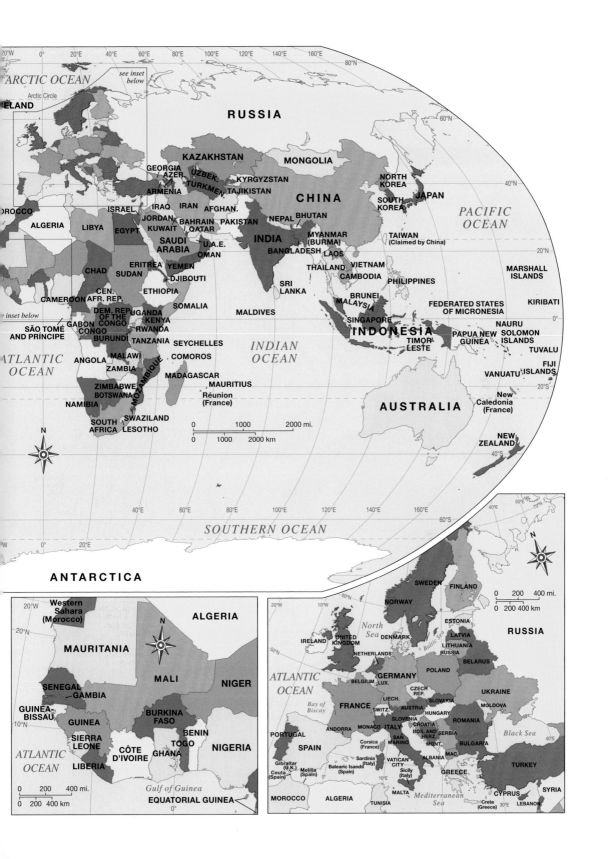

CHAPTER 1

Historical Background on Prohibition

Prohibition: An Overview

Charles Phillips

In the following viewpoint, Charles Phillips offers historical context for Prohibition. On January 16, 1920, the Eighteenth Amendment to the US Constitution went into effect, banning the manufacture, sale, and transportation (but not the consumption) of intoxicating beverages. This event initiated the era of US history known as Prohibition, which had long been advocated by the temperance movement and was already in effect in many states. But the expectations of its supporters were not fulfilled; far from reducing the evils caused by excessive drinking, Prohibition proved impossible to enforce and resulted in widespread law-breaking, corruption, and the rise of organized crime. In urban areas the sale of bootlegged liquor to otherwise law-abiding citizens was routine, and the involvement of gangsters often led to violence. Eventually, in 1933, the Eighteenth Amendment was repealed. Phillips is the author and co-author of numerous history books such as *What Every American Should Know About American History*, *The Macmillan Dictionary of Military Biography*, and *The Wages of History*.

Photo on previous page: This illustration of a poster by the Strengthen America Campaign is from the 1918 book *Why Prohibition!* by Charles Stelzle. (© **Fotosearch/ Getty Images.**)

SOURCE. Charles Phillips, "A Day to Remember: January 16, 1920," *American History*, February 2005. Copyright © 2005 by Weider History Group. All rights reserved. Reproduced by permission.

The night before the manufacture, transport and sale of alcoholic beverages became illegal in the United States of America, saloons and liquor stores held cut-rate sales. Nightclubs across the country staged mock funerals, some of them featuring coffins for the dying god John Barleycorn [a personification of liquor] whose effigy they would soon lay to rest. A rich habitué of the Park Avenue Club in New York City hosted a fancy formal at which the black-clad attendees tasted black caviar and toasted the coming of a society that banned drinking with champagne served in specially crafted black glasses. Newspaper reporters scoured the streets of New York and New Orleans and San Francisco looking for sensational accounts of last minute revelers before the Volstead Act, which was passed to provide for the enforcement of the 18th Amendment, went into effect on January 16, 1920.

The amendment itself had been ratified by a sufficient number of state legislatures to become the law of the land in 1919, plunging the country into what future U.S. President Herbert Hoover would call a "noble experiment" but what American citizens described more soberly as "Prohibition." The morning the Volstead Act went into effect, activists and supporters of Prohibition celebrated the victory of the "drys" over the "wets." The parades and extravagant rallies held in some cities, but especially in small towns throughout the land, boasted local politicians and celebrities who gave endless speeches extolling the virtues of abstinence and condemning the evils of demon rum, just as they had been doing for most of a century. In Washington, D.C., hundreds of congressmen attended the parade along with members of the Anti-Saloon League. Among the speakers was Secretary of State William Jennings Bryan, who in his many failed campaigns for president had become the spokesman for rural America.

"They are dead," came his famous clarion-call voice, "that sought the child's life. They are dead! They are dead! King Alcohol has slain more children than that Herod ever did." But now, he predicted, "The revolution that rocked the foundation of the Republic will be felt all over the earth."

A Long Time Coming

It was a change that had been a long time coming. Since the late 18th century, Americans occasionally banded together to try to persuade, cajole or force other Americans to quit drinking. Such temperance movements were cyclical, much like American religious revivals, and they usually appealed to evangelical, middle-class, native-born Protestants. In the two decades before the Civil War, temperance movements had some effect in reducing the amount of liquor Americans drank, which from Colonial times had been prodigious. By the 1840s, middle-class Americans no longer automatically entertained guests with a drink as they had in the previous century, and a country intent on developing its industry had begun to demand discipline among its workforce by banning the once frequent practice of drinking during special breaks on the job.

Alcohol consumption, however, began to increase again after the mid-19th century with the coming of German, Irish and other immigrants, whose drinking habits were European and who tended to congregate in saloons after work to socialize and discuss politics. In fact, by the late 19th century, saloons had become immigrant political institutions, the home of city bosses and political mechanics who found work for their ethnic kin in return for political loyalty and votes on Election Day. Prohibition, the heir to the temperance movement, took on a nativist cast and was often associated with progressive campaigns against corruption and bossism. It had become an attempt by middle-class Protestants, who felt their social and political dominance threatened by Catholic immigrants, urbanization and industrialization, to preserve the status quo.

The Distinction Between the Eighteenth Amendment and the Volstead Act

The Eighteenth Amendment was part of the US Constitution. Originally, the Constitution dealt only with the actions of the government—not individual citizens. Some later provisions affected individual actions, but only indirectly. For example, the Thirteenth Amendment, which prohibited slavery, meant that individuals could not own slaves, but no one could be sent to prison for "owning a slave" because the former slaves were no longer owned by anybody. The Eighteenth Amendment was the first attempt by the federal government to directly control citizens' conduct, a step many viewed as incompatible with the US principle of individual liberty. Although it prohibited manufacturing, selling, or transporting intoxicating liquor, the amendment alone did not mean people could be prosecuted for doing so. Violations of the Constitution can be stopped by government force, but there was no automatic penalty for them.

For this reason the Eighteenth Amendment contained a second clause that stated, "The Congress and the several States shall have concurrent power to enforce this article by appropriate legislation." A law was needed under which violators of the amendment could be arrested and punished. This law was officially titled the National Prohibition Act but was generally known as the Volstead Act, named for its congressional sponsor. It was passed by Congress in October 1919, a few months before the amendment went into effect. It superseded all existing state laws concerning liquor; defined "intoxicating beverages" (in a stricter way than most voters—who had not expected Prohibition to cover beer and wine—felt was necessary); established penalties for their manufacture, sale, and transportation; and regulated the production of alcohol for industrial, medicinal, and sacramental use. The Volstead Act did not, however, prohibit possession or consumption of liquor . . . except where state laws specified otherwise, it was not illegal to drink or to serve stockpiled liquor in homes.

By the 1870s, the temperance movement had also become associated with women's reform, because of the real threat that male drunkards posed to their wives and children. By common law, men controlled not only their own property but also that of their wives, and they could literally drink the family into destitution. Tales of wayward drunkards who physically abused their mates became standard fare in temperance tracts and at temperance meetings, where attendees might pledge total abstinence, place a capital T by their names and become Tee-Totalers. But the prominence of mostly middle-class women in the temperance movement of the late 19th century had also to do with a century's worth of social, economic and ideological developments.

As American society grew more industrial it developed what historians call the doctrine of separate spheres—the notion that a man's world was in the workplace and a woman's at home, but that both were of equal importance to family life. Male and female patterns of drinking began to diverge, as men did their social drinking outside the home and women, especially middle-class women, aspired to "true womanhood," which meant that while they were more delicate than men, they were also more morally refined. Once considered weak and immoral as a sex, they were now viewed as passionless and proper. It was their duty to see to the moral education and refinement of future generations, to use their roles as mothers to set good examples for their children and as ladies for their employees and less fortunate neighbors. With such a charge, most middle-class women quit drinking altogether.

When cheap immigrant labor provided middle-class families with domestics to handle the household drudgery, those morally upright women expanded their duties from managing the household to participating in charitable work in the community and, eventually, to taking up social issues such as abolition, suffrage and temperance.

On December 23, 1873, a Harvard-educated temperance advocate trained in homeopathic medicine, Dr. Diocletian Lewis, gave a temperance lecture in Hillsboro, Ohio, called "The Duty of Christian Women in the Cause of Temperance" that inspired local women to do as he said his mother had done when she was at wit's end over his father's drinking: invade saloons and shops that sold alcoholic beverages and persuade the owners to quit trafficking in drink. Throughout the winter, women in other towns followed their example, and after the *New York Times* picked up the story, thousands of women in hundreds of communities also organized into groups that invaded saloons and demanded pledges from bartenders, prayed, sang hymns, marched on the streets outside bars and drugstores, formed picket lines to prevent beverage deliveries, took down the names of patrons who ignored them and held mass temperance meetings. The short-lived Women's Temperance Crusade gave birth to the Woman's Christian Temperance Union (WCTU), which under the leadership of Frances Willard became the major vehicle for prohibition over the next two decades. Willard and others spread the organization into the South and West, where they became associated with the whole gamut of agrarian and radical Western reforms, from suffrage to the free-coinage of silver.

Pressure Groups

By 1890 more than half the counties in America contained WCTU organizations and a Prohibition Party had been formed to take the fight to the ballot box. Republicans uneasily adopted prohibition as a cause, while Democrats—outside the South—opposed it. Catholics, Germans (both Lutheran and Catholic), the Irish, eastern Europeans, the working class, urbanites, and those in counties where a disproportionate number of residents were male tended to vote against such amendments. Evangelical Protestant farmers tended to support them. Prohibition was a domestic issue and a small town and rural issue, all arenas in which the effects of excessive drinking tended to be most obvious.

The turn of the century witnessed the birth of the Anti-Saloon League. Prohibition Party gatherings could have been mistaken for revivals, but not so Anti-Saloon League meetings: They were all business. Like the Women's Temperance Crusade, the Anti-Saloon League began in Ohio, but unlike the women's temperance organizations, the Anti-Saloon League limited itself to one issue, prohibition, and would back any candidate, accept any proposal and support any group that advanced the cause in any fashion. The prototype of modern political pressure groups, the first league was formed in 1893 and became national in 1895 when the Ohio group merged with an organization in Washington, D.C.

The league depended not on volunteers but paid staff, mostly recruited from Protestant churches, and its general counsel and legislative superintendent, Wayne B. Wheeler, would actually write the Volstead Act. Though league members would use any argument to advance their cause, they concentrated not on individual drinkers or domestic issues, but on propaganda about the massive influence of the liquor "interests" in American—especially big-city—politics, and on economic arguments that claimed intemperance hurt worker productivity and that saloon districts discouraged growth. Knowing that prohibition seemed a way to instill discipline for emerging manufacturers confronting workers with traditional drinking habits, the league pitched its message to businessmen; John D. Rockefeller and Henry Ford, for example, were early and substantial patrons.

The Anti-Saloon League and other prohibitionists pointed to the growing incidence of radical protest from such organizations as the Industrial Workers of the World (IWW) and argued that it spread in step with liquor consumption. Blaming working-class drinking for industrial conflict was disingenuous at best, since almost all unions—including the IWW—insisted that their members remain sober, and many required a pledge to that effect in order to become a member.

But middle-class voters accepted the link between drinking and labor militancy because they did not wish to face the true source of the disorder: industrial growth. Meanwhile, unions and workers were hostile to the Anti-Saloon League not for its anti-alcohol message but for diverting attention from pressing issues of wealth and power. Industrialists, on the other hand, supported the league for just that reason, and most league leaders were members of the Republican Party. The result was that farmers and their wives voted rural areas dry under local option laws in order to protect their families from—and impose their sober Protestant-American values and work habits on—a "foreign" working class. Their native-born allies in the urban middle class voted their states dry to restore the order they believed was being disrupted by slum-dwelling alien anarchists. Once again, small towns proved the seedbed for the struggles over liquor, with nativism its engine of growth.

> Intended to create a nation of hardworking, sober, responsible citizens, Prohibition instead quickly transformed a nation of basically law-abiding citizens into a nation of lawbreakers.

Unexpected Results

By 1916, 21 state legislatures had outlawed saloons. That year, too, voters sent a "dry" majority to Congress. Those congressmen secured the passage of the 18th Amendment. Intended to create a nation of hardworking, sober, responsible citizens, Prohibition instead quickly transformed a nation of basically law-abiding citizens into a nation of lawbreakers. In the big cities, Prohibition had consistently been voted down, and it was in urban America that the new law was consistently violated. Neighborhood folk set up stills in their basements, brewing bathtub gin and other alcoholic concoctions. Within the neighborhoods, informal networks quickly developed, as grocers stocked the raw materials necessary to brew moonshine and former saloon-keepers, restaurant owners and ice cream and soft drink parlor operators helped local bootleggers distribute their wares. And that wasn't all. The friendly (and often corrupt) cop on the beat usually didn't pay the law any more heed than the citizens he was supposed to police. Routinely, he looked the other way. When higher authorities moved in, as they periodically did, to conduct surprise raids, typically the neighborhood was informed well in advance.

But the liquor business was not by nature a mom and pop affair. Even before the 18th Amendment went into effect on January 16, 1920, the urban underworld geared

Members of the Woman's Christian Temperance Union (WCTU) march on Washington in support of Prohibition in 1909. (© Topical Press Agency/Getty Images.)

up to supply what it knew would be a very lucrative demand for an illegal indulgence. And certain elements among the underworld realized that meeting the demand effectively would require a degree of organization hitherto unheard of in criminal circles. Thus the amendment's most enduring legacy to 20th-century America was what soon came to be called organized crime.

> The amendment's most enduring legacy to 20th-century America was what soon came to be called organized crime.

The mobsters moved in on the neighborhood operations. The gangsters, like those they preyed on, were immigrants, but they were ruthless and brutal, convinced that crime was the quickest route to riches in America. Such men tended to be at home with violence, and neighborhood bootlegging looked like a good, easy mark. They began by extorting protection money from the illegal traffickers and brutalizing the uncooperative. The terrorized bootleggers could hardly turn to the police for help, so they paid or gave up the business altogether. Within a short time, the gangs scrapped their protection schemes in favor of outright control of all liquor production and smuggling as well as distribution, including illicit bars, saloons and nightclubs, establishing a network of "speakeasies." Rival gangs, their members often no more than teenagers, battled each other for control of territory, making liberal use of sawed-off shotguns and the Thompson submachine guns ("tommy guns"), which in post-World War I America were available cheaply and in quantity as U.S. government surplus. Gangland slayings became commonplace, and terms like "hit" and "rub out" entered the language.

The mainstream press, pandering to its nativist, middle-class audience, tried to make a racial [ethnic] issue out of the crime wave that Prohibition created in the major American cities, and their headlines announced almost weekly still another Sicilian gang war or the discovery of yet one more illegal warehouse in this or that town's Little Italy. But the first well-known mobster in New York was an Englishman, Owney Madden, and the second a Jew, Arnold Rothstein. The Irish and Germans, too, had their own highly formidable gangs in almost every major city. The mobsters worked hand in glove with local political machines, securing votes and furnishing graft in return for protection from police interference. They poured their profits into clubs where jazz was played over the machine gun rat-tat-tat in the background. The deals struck in the mean streets of the 1920s steadily percolated up the power structure, until much of the country's political administration and law enforcement had been corrupted and co-opted.

A Changing Society

The year Prohibition went into effect was the year the U.S. Census documented that for the first time the number of people living in American cities had surpassed those living in rural areas. And in those cities industrialization was ushering in yet another change. In an economy that was producing more goods than it could sell, one that relied increasingly on advertising to foster new needs and create fresh markets for its surplus, pleasure-seeking became an approved pastime. The Broadway club life that developed from the cabarets of the 1890s began attracting young middle- and upper-class urbanites, who mixed with mobsters in a modern culture that exalted consumption and display rather than industry and thrift. Those thoroughly modern guys and dolls valued self-expression and individuality rather than sacrifice and family, and found fulfillment in leisure rather than work.

The Jazz Age was born in the speakeasies of Prohibition. Even before the Great Depression brought to office the Democrats who repealed the 18th Amendment in

April 1933, prohibitionists were losing all the ground it had taken them more than a century to gain, except in areas of the rural South and Midwest: Dry laws would linger on there in spots well into the second half of the 20th century.

A Senate Supporter of Prohibition Speaks in Its Favor

William S. Kenyon

Speaking in the Senate in favor of amending the US Constitution, Prohibition supporter William S. Kenyon argues that it would make no sense to ban the manufacture of whiskey as a means of conserving food and yet allow beer, because more foodstuff goes into beer than into whiskey; beer should be banned as well. Moreover, when men in the army and navy are not allowed to drink there is no reason why people at home should be permitted to do so, especially when they are being asked to conserve food. The goal of Prohibition is to abolish saloons, which Kenyon asserts breed corruption and crime and are responsible for more ruin and death than any war. The public conscience is aroused, he says, and the fight for Prohibition will go on until the saloons are banished. Kenyon was a US senator from Iowa.

SOURCE. William S. Kenyon, "Speech in the US Senate," *Congressional Record*, August 1, 1917. (Obtained from Stephen W. Stathis, "Eighteenth Amendment," *Landmark Debates in Congress: From the Declaration of Independence to the War in Iraq*. Washington, DC: CQ Press, 2009, pp. 269–274. Gale Virtual Reference Library.)

Mr. President, I want to take ten minutes to express a view or two on the pending subject; and in view of the fact that a bill at present in conference seeks to stop the manufacture of whisky as a food-conservation proposition, but not to stop the manufacture of beer. I desire to submit just an observation or two on that and other propositions in general relating to the subject. That part of my remarks will consist of questions which some proponents of the liquor traffic may perhaps answer in the further progress of this debate.

Why do we prohibit the boys in the Army and Navy from having booze and insist that those who remain at home shall have it?

If liquor is a bad thing for the boys in the trenches, why is it a good thing for those at home?

When they are willing to die for us, should we not be willing to go dry for them?

Will a sober nation not win the war quicker than a drunken nation?

When the food controller asks everyone in the country to conserve the food supply, why must the food supply going into beer be excepted?

Is it not as much waste of foodstuff to put it into beer as to put it into whisky? If more foodstuff goes into beer than into whisky, why do we prevent foodstuff going into whisky and permit it going into beer?

> If someone were taking as much foodstuff as goes into booze and dumping it into the sea, what would the people of the Nation say?

Will rebellions come in the cities, as we have been told, if the workers do not have their beer?

Sixty per cent of the Nation, territorially, is dry. Are the feelings of people living in that territory entitled to any consideration?

If the beer drinkers are going to rebel unless they get their beer, will the temperance people rebel unless they get temperance?

Does the rule only work one way?

Why do not the temperance people claim that they will rebel also? No one has heard any such thing from them, nor will anybody hear such thing.

The temperance people will be for the Nation no matter if beer and whisky be forced on them. Their patriotism does not depend on having their own way.

Is patriotism purchased by beer worthwhile anyway?

If someone were taking as much foodstuff as goes into booze and dumping it into the sea, what would the people of the Nation say?

If someone should advance the argument that this was necessary in order to appease certain people who believed in dumping foodstuffs into the sea, and that if they did not do it would arouse riots, would we accede to their request?

The War Effort Demands Prohibition

Is it reasonable to ask the temperance people of the country to conserve and save every particle of food and at the same time permit some of it to go into booze?

Is beer more essential to the American people than bread?

What kind of people are they in this country who are not willing to give up their liquor to help their country?

Is the food conservation to be for the benefit of the many, or is it to be limited in order that the few may have their drinks?

Have we reached a point in this country where the war cannot be won unless people who drink are permitted to tickle their stomachs with wines and beer?

Will beer patriots win the war anyhow?

Are the interests of brewers in this country more important than the winning of the war?

Are we willing to sacrifice everything in the country to win the war, except beer?

Prohibitionists march to the US Capitol in 1913 to show Congress their support for a constitutional amendment banning the production and sale of alcoholic beverages. (© Underwood & Underwood/Corbis.)

If the temperance forces in the Senate were responsible for delaying the food bill as charged by certain liquor-interest papers, why is it that the food bill has been delayed for three weeks after the temperance sections of the bill were settled?

With the great demand for labor in this country and the high wages, could there ever be a better time, as far as the laboring men are concerned, for the transition from a wet to a dry Nation?

When there is a shortage of labor in the important and necessary work to carry on the war, why waste labor in making booze?

If booze is essential to win the war, why stop selling it to the soldiers?

Mr. President, I have listened to the argument as to State rights; but I have discovered that the doctrine of

State rights absolutely vanishes in Congress whenever an appropriation is attached to a bill.

The advance in this country of the temperance cause has been due to the fight against the American saloon. That is what has been at the bottom of it. That has brought us to the issue of national prohibition.

This amendment is to give to the States the right to speak their desire on this question. Why should they not have such right? The American people are tired of saloons.

No one rises on this floor or elsewhere to defend the American saloon directly.

The Evil of the Saloon

The American saloon has no conscience. It never did a good act or failed to do a bad one.

It is a trap for youth; a destroyer for the old; a foul spawning place for crime; a corrupter of politics; knows no party; supports those men for office whom it thinks can be easiest influenced; has no respect for law or the courts; debauches city councils, juries, and everyone it can reach; is powerful in the unity of its vote, and creates cowards in office.

It flatters, tricks, cajoles, and deceives in order to accomplish its purpose; it is responsible for more ruin and death than all the wars the Nation has ever engaged in; has corrupted more politics, ruined more lives, widowed more women, orphaned more children, destroyed more homes, caused more tears to flow, broken more hearts, undermined more manhood, and sent more people to an early grave than any other influence in our land.

Its day has come. No subterfuge can long save it. It will be dragged into the open, the influences behind it stripped of their masks. A mighty public conscience is aroused, moving on rapidly, confidently, undismayed, and undeceived. Behind it are the churches of the Nation—Protestant and Catholic—schools, colleges, and homes. This public conscience is not discouraged by defeat or deceived by any cunning devices, by any shams or pretenses. Its cause is the cause of humanity, of righteousness, and God, Almighty fights with it.

> This fight . . . is going on in the Nation until the tear-producing, orphan-making, home-wrecking, manhood-debauching, character-destroying, hell-filling saloon business is banished from this country.

It has no desire to injure the saloon keeper. It would help him, but it asks no quarter of the saloon and it proposes to give none. The forces fighting the saloon are not composed of mollycoddies [pampered or over-protected men]. The most far-seeing business minds of the country are in the ranks.

Men will have to take their places in this fight. They cannot sit on the fence. This fight is no place for the political coward to stand between the lines. He will be shot from both directions.

No denunciation, no slurs, no jests on the floor of the Senate, no hurling of epithet, no cheap ribaldry in the cloakrooms will stop this fight. It is going on in Congress, and it is going on in the Nation until the tear-producing, orphan-making, home-wrecking, manhood-debauching, character-destroying, hell-filling saloon business is banished from this country. The American saloon is just as certainly doomed as slavery is doomed.

A saloonless Nation means an efficient Nation, better able to cope with any problem threatening it from without or within.

Opponents React to the Ruling That the Eighteenth Amendment Is Constitutional

New York Times

There were a number of legal challenges to the constitutionality of the Eighteenth Amendment and the Volstead Act, and in 1920 the US Supreme Court issued a single opinion countering these objections and declaring the new law valid. As explained in the following 1920 *New York Times* article, the first news report of this decision was inaccurate and opponents of Prohibition celebrated, thinking that the law had been overturned. When they learned the truth, leaders of the opposition expressed their belief that the Supreme Court made a bad decision that would damage the government and might lead to attempts to ban other things, such as smoking and Sunday sports. They predicted—accurately, as it turned out— that Prohibition could not be enforced and liberal voters would eventually bring about the restoration of personal liberty.

SOURCE. "False Report Elates Wets," *New York Times*, June 8, 1920.

Misinterpretation of the decision of the United States Supreme Court upholding the constitutionality of the Eighteenth Amendment and the Volstead Enforcement act gave anti-prohibitionists in the city a few moments of joy yesterday afternoon, but within five minutes their joy was turned to gloom when they found that the decision of the court really put a legal quietus on the sale of liquors for beverage purposes.

The first "flash" of the decision received in this city from Washington indicated that the amendment and the enforcement act had been declared invalid, and in a few seconds the report was being telephoned all over the city. Saloons and cafés in the financial district were the first to receive the false report, and patrons of these places hurried into the streets to carry it to others. Eventually it was being telephoned to every oasis along the mid-Broadway section, and spread like wildfire to the saloons on the east and west sides and to Harlem and the Bronx.

There were many exchanges of "Well, here's how," while the report was gaining ground among the resorts of the illicit purveyors, but it was not long until the true significance of the decision reached the public. Then the festivities in the saloons and restaurants which had received the first report turned to somewhat funereal ceremonies, and the talk drifted to discussion about "personal liberty" and the like.

Representatives of the liquor and brewing interests in the city kept in touch with the local headquarters of the organizations opposed to prohibition from early in the morning, for word went out in the latter part of last week that the Supreme Court would hand down its decision yesterday. Saloon-keepers, who had been informed that the liquor interests here would receive the decision by telephone as soon as it was handed down, gathered in the several headquarters established by the brewers and the liquor interests, nervously puffing cigars while they awaited word from Washington.

When the word came those gathered in the anti-prohibitionists' headquarters made no effort to conceal their disgust as they quickly left to begin the work of winding up their affairs as purveyors of "wet goods."

Opposition Leaders Refuse to Comment

William D. Guthrie, who was associated with Elihu Root in the fight in the Federal courts to have the prohibition law declared unconstitutional, when asked last night if he desired to make a statement, said: "I never make statements on such matters." Mr. Root is on his way to Europe. When Emory R. Buckner, a member of his firm, was asked if he had any comment to make, he replied: "No. There is no comment to make."

Governor Edward I. Edwards of New Jersey, who has openly advocated the setting aside of the prohibition law, when informed of the decision of the Supreme Court at his office in Jersey City, said: "I decline to make any comment until I see the decision."

Christian W. Feigenspan, President of the United States Brewers' Association, when asked for an opinion on the decision in his office in Newark, N.J., said:

"I have not read the opinion, and, therefore, I have nothing to say on the matter, except that I understand the Supreme Court has rendered the decision, and that is the court of last resort."

Mr. Feigenspan, who is the head of C. Feigenspan, Inc., brewers, was the complainant in one of the suits brought before the Supreme Court to test the validity of the Eighteenth Amendment and the Volstead act.

Statement Declares Law Cannot Be Enforced

The Association Opposed to National Prohibition issued a statement, which read in part:

The United States Supreme Court has held that the Eighteenth Amendment is legally a part of the Constitution of the United States. Now that it is a part of the fundamental law of the land, the only way to get rid of it is to repeal it.

> 'A statute which cannot be enforced is a dead statute, and its death weakens the whole body of statutory law.'

When personal life and living are involved no decision of any court can be final. The opinion of the body politic must prevail and that opinion has yet to be expressed. It is not our purpose to reargue the legality of the Eighteenth Amendment—that has been decided once and for all. Whether, or not, the highest court of the republic has outlived its usefulness will depend on what the opinion of the voters of the republic may be as recorded at the polls. Meantime, it must be borne in mind that prohibition has never been capable of enforcement in this country and the indications are that it never will be.

A statute which cannot be enforced is a dead statute, and its death weakens the whole body of statutory law.

In our opinion, the decision of the United States Supreme Court is a menace and not a hope. The Eighteenth Amendment violates every principle for which the soldiers of the American Revolution fought. The United States Supreme Court may not undo those principles without undoing the Republic. So long as the Eighteenth Amendment is a part of the Constitution of the United States, it invites every meal-ticket reformer to start an anti-prohibition movement of this, that or the other kind. The way to stop the meals and stop the reformers is by a general union of the intelligent liberal forces of the Republic.

Personal liberty, constitutional liberty and anti-prohibition organizations whose mainspring of action is principle, and not pelf [riches], will join in a great national liberal movement in this country which will put the fanatics and the meal-ticket reformers on the run and out of business.

Some See Danger of New Crusades

Edward B. Cochens, chairman of the National Executive Committee of the Fraternal Order of Camels, the headquarters of which are in the Fitzgerald Building in this city, which is said to have 200,000 members with "caravans," or local organizations in every city in the country, declared that opponents of prohibition would keep up the fight to abolish the law regardless of the decision of the Supreme Court. [He said:]

Men participate in an anti-Prohibition parade in 1925. Opponents of Prohibition and the Eighteenth Amendment took their fight to the US Supreme Court on several occasions. (© FPG/ Hulton Archive/Getty Images.)

I consider the decision of the Supreme Court the most drastic of any yet made by that court in the history of our country. . . .

It menaces the equilibrium that exists between the Federal and State Governments, and will cause to exist in the future such a strain between them that, in the confusion that will follow, it will bring about constant irritation and friction, which will menace the very framework of government itself.

The program of the people who brought about the ratification of the eighteenth amendment will be continued, and their efforts unsatisfied. They will now attempt to stamp out the use of tobacco, abolish Sunday motion picture performances, Sunday theatres, wholesome sports on Sunday, and, as William Jennings Bryan says, will attempt to amend the Constitution in favor of a single standard of morals.

'There will be no limit to the use of the Constitution for mere legislative purposes. The gates are open.'

They will also, as a Presbyterian synod stated in convention, amend the Constitution to have the Bible recognized as the one authority, etc. There will be no limit to the use of the Constitution for mere legislative purposes. The gates are open, and with that decision as a precedent they can accomplish any oppression that they desire.

The decision simply means that the fight will now go to the people, who alone have the power to bring about a change.

William H. Hirst, counsel for the New York Brewers' Association, said:

"Our only hope now rests in the action of some future Congress, which may change the official definition of intoxicating liquors."

College Officials Express a Belief That Prohibition Is a Success

World League Against Alcoholism

The World League Against Alcoholism conducted a survey in 1922 in which prominent people were asked whether they felt Prohibition was working. The resulting publication was not a statistical survey; it simply consisted of the comments of respondents who favored Prohibition. Among them were many college presidents and professors, most of who said either that drinking among students had stopped or that they were confident it soon would end. Considering the extent of the public's disregard for the law, it is possible that the students at some colleges managed to conceal the extent of alcohol consumption; in any case, most officials had an overly optimistic view of the law's success. Ernest H. Cherrington, who edited this collection, was a leading temperance journalist and activist.

SOURCE. Ernest H. Cherrington, ed., *A Cloud of Witnesses.* Washington, DC: World League Against Alcoholism, 1923?, pp. 36–38, 42–54.

The banishment of the saloon and the outlawry of the liquor traffic, even under the imperfect enforcement of the amendment and the statute, has proved a blessing to the home, to the father, mother and child. The money saved has provided better food, clothing and housing, and therefore better health and morals; while the decrease of drunkenness has tended to restore domestic peace and happiness. —*Professor George Elliott Howard, Department of Political Science and Sociology, University of Nebraska [Lincoln, Nebraska].*

While it is undoubtedly difficult to enforce at present in large cities, where there is still a strong hangover sentiment against it, I believe that President [Warren G.] Harding has hit the nail on the head when he said that "in another generation I believe that liquor will have disappeared not merely from our politics but from our memories." . . . My prediction is that prohibition will bring converts to it and very rapidly. —*Irving Fisher, Professor of Political Economy, Yale University [New Haven, Connecticut].*

In spite of exhibitions of lawlessness here and there, the beneficent effects of prohibition are being felt more and more. Literally, millions of persons have quietly given up drink altogether, thus adding to their happiness and prosperity. The American saloon, with its baneful "treating" habit and all evil concomitants—malignant cancer that it was, has been cut out of our body politic. Best of all, a generation of American boys and girls are growing up in our midst who will soon come to maturity without the taint of alcohols. —*Professor Rockwell H. Hunt, Dean of the Graduate School, University of Southern California [Los Angeles, California].*

Five years from now most of those who indulge heavily in liquor at the present moment will have forgotten about it. It will cease to be smart and clever to become drunken. Already there is apparent a recovery from the first reaction against prohibition, and people are ceasing to talk about drinking, or to make a display of their ability to secure liquor for consumption.

> The rising generation will not know the taste of liquor

The rising generation will not know the taste of liquor; they will not see it being consumed in public places; they will not form a taste for it or a habit of indulging in order to conform to group practice, and so they will have no wish for it. But it will take a generation completely to eliminate the desire for alcohol and practice of ridiculing prohibition and glorifying alcoholic indulgence. —*M.V. O'Shea, Professor of Education, University of Wisconsin [Madison, Wisconsin].*

A Passing Phase

Prohibition is the best thing that has happened in recent years in this country. We have a certain percentage of students and perhaps a few of the faculty who are still in the playful stage of life and who are amusing themselves by fretfully defying the law with the delusion that they are deriving entertainment in the process. I think this is a passing phase and that prohibition is here to stay and to succeed. —*President Ray Lyman Wilbur, Stanford University [Stanford, California].*

I would say that there is less drinking among college students in this part of the country than ever before within the memory of man. When they do drink, the stuff now sold has most alarming effects, but as a habit, drinking has very greatly decreased since the introduction of the new law. To me, it is a great satisfaction that students can now go up and down the streets of our city without being solicited at every corner by the open saloon. —*W.H.P. Faunce, President, Brown University [Providence, Rhode Island].*

It is very difficult to get a true expression of the opinion of educated men and college students with regard to prohibition. Usually their real opinion is hidden or disguised under a comic mask. Nevertheless, I believe that the great majority are heartily in favor of prohibition in spite of the evils with which its introduction has been accompanied. What seems to me to be only a small minority are in favor of beer and light wines, but even those composing this minority would be in favor of the "bonedry" as opposed to the "wide open."—*C.H. Clapp, President, State University of Montana, Missoula, Montana.*

In theory, American prohibition is wholly commendable, marks a long step in advance in the promotion of human welfare, has already immeasurably benefited the United States, and should by all means be retained.

In practice, however, I would say that in my judgment, circumstances conspired to put the amendment into the United States constitution from five to ten years too soon. Its enforcement is meeting with three formidable difficulties:

> The present reaction against the law will steadily decrease as its enforcement becomes more universal and the people more law-abiding.

First, the natural hostility of millions of drinkers whose personal habits and desires have been suddenly and harshly interfered with.

Second, its enforcement, difficult at all times, has been undertaken during the years of universal revolt against all restrictions and conventions caused by the shake-up of the World War.

Third, and most important, its enforcement has been entrusted to two mutually jealous agencies, namely, the federal government and the local authorities.

In such states as Virginia, the latter is the most serious obstacle to enforcement. When United States revenue officers take up the task, the local officers not only feel absolved of responsibility, but are almost sure to lose sympathy and refuse cooperation.

I believe, however, that the present reaction against the law will steadily decrease as its enforcement becomes more universal and the people more law-abiding. Personally, I have no fear that the amendment will be repealed or its enforcement nullified. —*Henry Louis Smith, President of Washington and Lee University, Lexington, Virginia.*

Results Justify the Law

The faculty and students of Willamette University, I am confident, have but one judgment concerning National Prohibition: it is wholly desirable both in theory and fact, and the results of the National Amendment thus far justify the law and promise still better results in the future.

In the University we have never been greatly troubled by the students using liquor, although in former years we have occasionally been obliged to discipline students for drinking. Now this is a thing of the past, the city is quieter, the general tone of the community has improved, and that dark spot in the educational atmosphere is practically eliminated. Anything which tends to weaken the enforcement of this law is a serious thrust at all respect of order and a weakening of a most desirable advance in general progress.

Were the question to be put to a vote of faculty and students in Willamette University, there would assuredly not be 1 per cent desire a return to the old order. —*C.G. Doney, President of Willamette University, Salem, Oregon.*

I am sure that every member of our faculty and practically every one of our students is glad that the saloon has disappeared. There are possibly a few of our faculty and a considerably larger proportion of our students who regret that they cannot get liquor to drink when they want it. There is a little feeling that it was unwise to make prohibition so drastic and possibly this latter feeling is stronger than I apprehend. I am sure that among my acquaintances outside of the college there are many who greatly regret the severity of the present restrictions.

Occasionally, a few of our students get hold of some liquor, but since prohibition went into effect I think there have been no cases of drunkenness and where there has been some drinking it has been confined to a very few men, not over four or five at a time, and these occasions have been extremely rare. We do not have the trouble with drink here that many of the large eastern colleges do. —*Charles S. Howe, President, Case School of Applied Science, Cleveland, Ohio.*

The only comment that I can make is that which is based upon personal impression, rather than upon any scientific accumulation of data, which ould be difficult to secure.

My reluctant conviction is, however, that the code of the college can only be kept about so far in advance of the code of the social group from which the undergraduate body is drawn, and that, although there has probably never been so little use of liquor within the college as at the present time, the restraint is due wholly to an undergraduate sense of responsibility for the college name and not from any conviction in regard to the merits of the prohibition law. I am not sure what conclusion should be drawn from this fact, but I am quite clear that unless the prohibition law becomes more effective in fact, and unless the spirit of lawlessness in the country at large becomes subdued and the violation of the law becomes less, neither Dartmouth nor any other college will be able permanently to maintain a condition largely contradictory to the social conditions with which the men are familiar in their home communities or in their social contacts outside the college.

In the last analysis, I think that the sentiment of the faculty and the undergraduate body on the subject of prohibition will not be very different from that of the constituency which makes up the better and more progressive communities representative of American life. My great concern for the college is that there seems to be no adequate support for the theory of the prohibition law which will enable it to be sufficiently observed in practice to make its results avoid the appearance of futility. In other words, I would prefer, if forced to the alternative, to have our men grow up with increased rather than lessened respect for the law, even if this involved some changed conditions in the prohibition requirements which make the law more possible of enforcement. —*Ernest M. Hopkins, President, Dartmouth College, Hanover, New Hampshire.*

Dartmouth students drink during a Winter Carnival a few years after the repeal of Prohibition. In 1923 the college's president expressed his concern that students refraining from alcohol consumption was contradictory to social norms. (© Peter Stackpole/Time & Life Pictures/Getty Images.)

Conflicting Views

I hear on various sides the statement that prohibition is a failure: that conditions are worse than ever before and the like. On the contrary, I have read with great satisfaction an article in the Sunday *Times* in January by a man who was appointed from England to investigate conditions throughout the United States. As you know, the *Times* is not for Prohibition and the writer of that article is not an advocate of prohibition. He goes into details which show that conditions are far better than the liquor propaganda seeks to indicate. That is my own conviction.

I find that some good men are misled by liquor propaganda and are expressing the idea that prohibition tends toward lawlessness. However, the liquor business has been nothing but lawless as long as I can remember.

The same forces which have brought about the Constitutional Amendment will fight through to the enforcement of that article of the Constitution and the laws which support it. No one need suppose that the enormous weight of sentiment which carried the amendment through forty-five states will fail to carry this enterprise through successfully. —*William Lowe Bryan, President, Indiana University, Bloomington, Indiana.*

Students realize that no law can be enforced beyond the willingness of the people to obey the law. Millions of people did not favor the abolition of slavery and it died out slowly under forms like compulsory labor and the like. It will take some time for the sentiment of all the people to be in favor of obeying the law abolishing liquors. College students as a body will help to enforce it as they helped to secure it. —*Edwin E. Sparks, President Emeritus. Pennsylvania State College, State College, Pennsylvania.*

College sentiment here as elsewhere generally favors prohibition as a theory, but many thoughtful people fail to sympathize with the present enactments of the United States on this question. . . .

The opinion of most colleges regarding prohibition as a fact is that there is no such fact. It is a matter of common and universal knowledge that the present laws are not enforced and most people think they cannot be enforced. Others think that these laws may be obeyed in some remote time in the future after education has done its work. The opinion of these men is that the task of prohibitionists today is not different from what it has been in all past years, namely, to build up a sentiment opposed to drinking.

Student sentiment does not regard the violation of the present prohibition law as any great offense. They apply toward these laws the same principle that they apply to many of the regulations of school, which is that the existence of the regulation is an invitation to a student to violate it.

Because of these facts the problem of dealing with drinking and drunkenness among students has not in any degree been lessened by present prohibition laws. I am personally of the opinion that these problems are even more difficult and more acute than they were before the passage of national prohibition. I presume every college that is trying to assume responsibility for the moral conduct of the students is finding the greatest possible difficulty in handling this question. —*J.H. Kirkland, President, Vanderbilt University, Nashville, [Tennessee].*

Great Benefits

The faculty and students of Mercer University are unanimous in their approval of Prohibition, both in theory and in fact. The law is being enforced better with each passing month. The reaction following the war resulted in an increase of violations of the Volstead act, but these violations are now being limited to the worst element in the so-called upper classes and the worst elements in the lower classes. —*Rufus W. Weaver, President, Mercer University, Macon, Georgia.*

I do not know that it is profitable to discuss the theory of prohibition. It is beginning to be a fact and is more of a fact as time continues. There isn't any question but that college administration is easier under present conditions. The drink problem in student life has almost disappeared and will soon be a thing of the past. Having been for many years in active work with students, I can say without hesitation that the benefits of prohibition to American colleges and universities have been great.

> The drink problem in student life has almost disappeared and will soon be a thing of the past.

Lest I should be misunderstood I want to add that the problem has not entirely disappeared, but with continued vigilance it will [disappear] and that will be a blessing. —*H.M. Gage, President, Coe College, Cedar Rapids, Iowa.*

Prohibition seems to me entirely right in theory and entirely right in enactment in view of existing conditions and the desired welfare of society. Its enactment I have not the slightest doubt will stand and obedience to it in due time [will] become well established. The thing most to be regretted at the present moment is the attitude of many excellent citizens in more or less condoning disregard of law and assisting to spread the idea that prohibition enactment, rather than lawlessness, is the cause of the evils now afflicting us. —*W.H. Demarest, President, Rutgers College, New Brunswick, New Jersey.*

The result of the prohibition years is a clear demonstration that both in "theory and in fact" it is working well from a university standpoint. The whole problem of discipline has been both simplified and lessened; the morale of student bodies has been improved and the number of men dropped because of misconduct greatly reduced. What is true of the university is also true of the community in almost as marked a degree. Even lax enforcement of the law cannot obscure its value. I am very confident that a large percentage of my colleagues upon the faculty would subscribe to these statements. *—Stanley Coulter, Acting Chairman of the Faculty, Purdue University, Lafayette, Indiana.*

Prohibition Proved Impossible to Enforce

Malcolm F. Willoughby

In the following viewpoint, Malcolm F. Willoughby explains that when Prohibition went into effect, the authorities did not expect difficulty in enforcing it, but the assumption that the law would be obeyed proved false. From the first day on, it was consistently broken. It became fashionable to drink, even among people who were previously law-abiding, and respect for law in general declined. Liquor was manufactured in homes and by illicit stills or was smuggled in from other countries. Gangsters and racketeers were often involved; eventually organized crime took over, aided by the corruption of officials who took bribes. Smuggling by sea, known as rum-running, was common and was combated by the US Coast Guard. But despite all the government's efforts, liquor remained widely available. Willoughby was a commander in the US Coast Guard.

SOURCE. Malcolm F. Willoughby, "The 'Nobel Experiment,'" *Rum War at Sea*. US Coast Guard, 1964, pp. 11–19.

As Prohibition went into effect on 17 January 1920, enforcement personnel were ready. . . . Authorities expected few violations, however, for penalties under the Volstead Act were severe. Even the wets expected that prohibition would prohibit. Naturally, a large segment of the populace had prepared for the event by hoarding. Rather frantic private buying had been going on for months. As the day approached, there was a country-wide rush to buy up the existing supply. Little was wasted.

On the morning of the first day of prohibition, agents seized trucks loaded with liquor in Peoria, Ill., and in New York City; they issued

> "Once liquor was legally banned, it seemed to gain in desirability."

12 warrants for the arrest of violators in New York, and raided stills in several other large cities. From this point forward until 5 December 1933, when the amendment was finally repealed, the prohibition law was broken on a wide-spread scale during every minute of that 14-year period, despite everything the Federal Government and its agencies could do in an effort to prevent it.

Once liquor was legally banned, it seemed to gain in desirability. The old drinkers were not to be denied if they could help it; new drinkers discovered something akin to a thrill in possessing and partaking of the forbidden spirits. A person who was able to get some liquor was looked upon by himself and his friends as "smart." Liquor could not be sold openly, of course, but there were thousands all over the country who risked arrest by selling it under cover, and so speakeasies sprang up like mushrooms. The business became very lucrative. Citizens who were otherwise law-abiding patronized the speakeasies along with the less meticulous, and thus became lawbreakers.

The younger generation of boys and girls caught the spirit, and drinking became the "thing to do." Women became much more interested in what had been largely a men's province. Boys and girls in colleges became good customers, and bootleggers and speakeasies in college vicinities did a brisk business. Social conditions in the schools and colleges deteriorated considerably. The same was true of the older group, and country clubs and many other organizations had a new lease on life. Not only did all this involve law-breaking, but it seemed to engender a wider contempt for law generally at all levels of society.

> Boys and girls in colleges became good customers, and bootleggers and speakeasies in college vicinities did a brisk business.

Violence and Corruption

Liquor came from three principal sources. There was that manufactured in many thousands of homes; that which was produced in thousands of stills, chiefly in the back country but also in cities and towns; and that which entered the country from outside its borders. The best quality of liquor, of course, came from the third source.

The various law enforcement agencies kept a watch for liquor being illegally transported by truck, train or ship, raided hotels, clubs, speakeasies, and other establishments, and made arrests. These activities were not always peaceful. In the first 12 months, prohibition officials claimed that one Federal agent and one civilian had been killed. The Bureau of Internal Revenue announced in April 1926 that up to then 89 civilians and 47 enforcement personnel (including two coast guardsmen) had been killed. By October 1930, 200 civilians and 86 prohibition agents had been killed according to one report. The Wickersham Commission differed somewhat, reporting that, by the beginning of 1931, the figures were 144 and 60 respectively. These numbers did not include State enforcement personnel, or officers of counties, cities, and towns, or killings by such personnel. Probably three times as many killings occurred at the local level. Many shootings were in self defense, but, regardless of the "merits" of the cases, these killings aroused much public indignation.

The Department of Justice made no particular preparations to handle violators of the Volstead Act; only a relatively few cases of this sort were expected. But in only a few months the Federal courts throughout the country were literally overwhelmed by the number of cases awaiting trial; penitentiaries could hardly hold the rum runners, bootleggers, and others who had been arrested. . . .

> The Federal courts throughout the country were literally overwhelmed . . . penitentiaries could hardly hold the rum runners, bootleggers, and others who had been arrested.

While a majority of cases were handled honestly, bribery and corruption were prevalent. U.S. attorneys across the country spent at least 44 percent of their time on dry law cases, and in many States much more. The U.S. courts staggered under the load. Enforcement by many States was dilatory. . . .

Corruption among some of the prohibition agents themselves is a matter of public record, as well as corruption in other agencies. Certainly, the numerous and generous offers from brewing and distilling interests, rum runners, bootleggers, and speakeasies were highly tempting to law enforcement personnel. That many succumbed to the temptations is not surprising. . . .

One of the most important agencies concerned with law enforcement was the U.S. Coast Guard. As a result of its additional duties to prevent smuggling of liquor into the United States from the sea, a rapid expansion of its facilities and personnel was required. . . . Its personnel were almost entirely immune from the temptations of the day, though there were some exceptions. In the first 2 years a few temporary warrant officers and enlisted

Smugglers Found Creative Ways to Evade the Law

In direct contradiction of the statements persistently circulated by the Anti-Saloon League, Dr. M.S. Gregory, director of the Bellevue Hospital [New York City], reports today [May 1920] that the number of patients suffering from over-indulgence in alcohol is daily increasing. The report forms the basis of a public attack upon the Federal authorities responsible for the enforcement of Prohibition.

The extent to which smuggling has developed is illustrated by a report from Detroit describing how electrically driven torpedoes loaded with whisky are being sent daily across the Detroit River from the Canadian to the American shore. The torpedoes submerge 100 feet and take 5 minutes to cross the river. They are emptied on the American side, ballasted with water, and sent back to Canada for reloading.

SOURCE: Daily Mail (London), May 10, 1920.

men were convicted of scheming with rum runners and bootleggers. In 1925 the crews of two patrol boats were court-martialed for assisting or protecting smugglers. There were a few other isolated cases. Far more numerous were the instances of attempted bribery which were unsuccessful.

There were instances, too, in the Customs Service and among other Government employees, and State, county, and municipal officials. These were the cases that made the news; routine and honest enforcement rarely did so, and such publicity gave false impressions. The great majority of Government agents were honest, conscientious people who endeavored to do their assigned duties according to the book regardless of their personal feelings or reactions about an obviously unpopular law. . . .

Organized Crime

Gradually, the most famous drinking and dancing resorts came under the domination of the big-shot criminal element.

This element grew rapidly and soon became wealthy. It acquired control over the flow of liquor into the city. It dictated distribution and sale, financed night clubs, operated syndicates, and directed the New York liquor wars. It had liquor and other alliances which became literally country-wide. . . . In large measure these men were responsible for the deaths of hundreds of bootleggers and gangsters through various means but especially through the employment of gunmen to whom such work was merely a means of livelihood.

> [The] upsurge of the underworld as a result of prohibition was undoubtedly its most vicious development.

This upsurge of the underworld as a result of prohibition was undoubtedly its most vicious development. Not only did it advance the old-time thugs and racketeers in their chosen professions, but it brought in and developed thousands of new ones. This was the element which, in large part, eventually controlled the great inflow of liquor from the sea, which was to become one of the greatest problems of the period and the particular concern of the U.S. Coast Guard.

But the interests of these barons of crime did not end with the liquor traffic itself; there were many corollary activities which included narcotics traffic, gambling, racketeering, extortion, robbery, prostitution, and murder. Even within the high-up criminal element itself things were not always peaceful. Hijacking and doublecrossing were almost common. These men were terrorists in their field, and many of the enforcement agents avoided getting mixed up with them. To bring such people to book was pretty much a major operation.

When they were taken to court, the perpetrators of widespread crime were ably defended by skilled, well-paid, and unscrupulous lawyers who, in innumerable instances, succeeded in impressing courts which seemed very willing to be impressed.

The story of the rise of these gangsters and racketeers, of whom Al Capone and "Legs" Diamond were perhaps the most famous, the fortunes which they amassed, and the intrigues, murders, and doublecrossing in which they engaged, constituted a shameful byproduct of prohibition. . . .

At any rate, during the "Noble Experiment," as President [Herbert] Hoover called it, liquor was profitably dispensed all over New York City, and speakeasies and other places in the city where it was sold numbered high in the thousands. In the other major cities the same was generally true in proportion to the size of the population. There were raids, arrests, and court convictions by the thousands, but the flow of liquor in these cities was never stemmed or even perceptibly retarded. . . .

Sources of Liquor

In the first few years of the dry era, illicit distillers produced whiskey of a sort, but after 1925 most shifted over to making alcohol. This was easier and more profitable and storing was unnecessary. Production assumed large proportions, and eventually this source exceeded all others combined. There were many hundreds of thousands of stills operating day and night across this broad land. One thinks of stills as typically in the mountains and backwoods. They were there, in quantity, but also in the cities and towns. The stills produced not only whiskey and alcohol, but a lot of money for their operators. They ranged from crude homemade devices to distilleries capable of making 2,000 gallons a day; the large ones often enjoyed excellent police and political protection.

In the larger cities the producers were often controlled by the gang leaders in a well organized operation. The leaders sometimes provided the stills and materials, paid the operators a wage or a share of the profit, collected the alcohol regularly by truck, and sold [it] to wholesale bootleggers. Alcohol thus produced became "gin" after a little treatment by the consumer. Moonshiners in many country areas were also controlled by hoodlums and criminal gangs with connections in the big cities.

As would be expected, prohibition agents seized a tremendous number of stills. In the first 5 years alone, the seizures totaled 696,933. It was estimated in 1926 that at least 500,000 persons were engaged in this type of distilling. With all this widespread activity one might well ask how the authorities allowed it, but it should be remembered that at no time did the Prohibition Bureau have more than 2,300 field agents; protection was widespread; and thus it was an almost impossible situation.

It can be readily appreciated that most of the liquor produced by these various means could not be classed as good. Yet, a great deal of good liquor was available. Most of this, along with much liquor of poor quality, found its way into the country from outside of the borders. All of this had to be smuggled in either from across the Canadian or Mexican borders, or from the sea. Tremendous quantities flowed in from Canada, particularly through Detroit. These were chiefly the concern of the customs men and prohibition agents, though smuggling across the St. Lawrence River and the Great Lakes was also the concern of the Coast Guard.

Those smuggling spirits in from Canada and Mexico had certain advantages. Liquor was not contraband until it had actually crossed the border into the United States. Smugglers by land had 6,000 miles of border country in which to choose their point of entry. From Canada there were more than 400 reasonably good roads, plus 150 which were passable, and a good number of trails. From Mexico, the figure can be divided by about four. . . . In the earlier years there were only about 35 agents for the Mexican border and scarcely 100 for the Canadian boundary. Even with enforcement efforts at their best, it was like trying to stem a flood with a rake. And the flood started within 2 weeks of the advent of prohibition.

Automobiles and trucks took the supplies in over the border roads, while boats transported liquor across rivers and lakes. On the American side, they were usually met and escorted by gunmen. This meant some shooting, of course. Eight guards had been killed and 23 civilians, mostly smugglers, had been slain by the guards by late 1929. Liquor was even smuggled in by air, and railroad freight cars were convenient when railroad employees were cooperative for a liberal remuneration.

These smuggling operations, as well as those on salt water, were not haphazard activities. The entire operations, from importation to final dispensers, were largely controlled by the organized gangsters and racketeers. Large sums of money were expended for the most modern and efficient equipment to defeat the plans of the Coast Guard and other enforcement agencies.

For a few years the combinations worked quite harmoniously together, but rivalries developed, hijacking became frequent, gang wars broke out. Syndicates became bigger, fewer, and more powerful. . . .

Rum Runners

While rum runners were active all along the Atlantic seaboard and the Gulf coast, there were five principal points where entry by sea was chiefly concentrated. The largest

and most important was, of course, the New York area, including Long Island and the New Jersey shores. It was in these waters that Rum Row was established. A subsidiary Rum Row existed at times off Boston. A great deal of liquor was run into the country in Florida waters, partly because of the proximity of Cuba and the British-owned Bahama Islands. And much found its way between the Virginia Capes [Cape Charles and Cape Henry, forming the entrance to the Chesapeake Bay], and also into the New Orleans market.

The usual procedure was to load fairly large vessels with the cargoes of liquor at the various foreign ports of supply and depart for points off the coast where the vessels were anchored. These were the supply, or mother ships. The larger ones were mostly New England or Canadian fishing schooners, able to carry one to three

Moonshiners ran vast and complex operations to supply speakeasies such as this one in New York City in 1933. (© Margaret Bourke-White/Time & Life Pictures/Getty Images.)

thousand cases on a trip. They were good sea boats and could ride out almost anything the weatherman ordered. But there were also steam trawlers, converted yachts, tramp steamers, and old windjammers. Rum Row consisted of a motley collection of craft of many types.

Contact with shore was made through smaller boats. These came out to the rum ships from shore, lay alongside, took on their cargoes, paid for the load, and returned to shore where they were unloaded. In the earlier days Rum Row was only just beyond the 3-mile limit, and boats of every description went out for their supplies. Liquor was sold to all comers. Even rowboats and small boats with outboard motors were used. Gradually, speedboats came into preference, and before long they predominated. As time went on, and Rum Row was pushed outside the 12-mile zone by international agreement, larger and faster craft became the rule. . . .

The smuggling of liquor from the sea began in a small way but grew to immense proportions. At first, the enforcement of the prohibition law fell chiefly upon the customs and prohibition agents. Through 1920 and 1921, customs officers seized contraband liquor in increasing quantities both along the borders and along the shores. Prohibition agents could intercept liquor being landed on the wharves of New York and other large coastal cities to some extent, and in some ports they had boats of their own to catch the small craft operating in local waters. The task, however, proved far beyond their capabilities. After about 2 years of the dry law, [Federal Prohibition] Commissioner [John F.] Kramer said that prohibition enforcement was a failure due to the antagonism of the people.

It soon fell squarely upon the U.S. Coast Guard to suppress the smuggling from the sea. . . .

With its fleet of cutters for offshore work and a large number of small craft for coastal and inshore activity, this was the logical service for the duty of enforcement on salt water.

From the beginning to the end, the Coast Guard undertook to wage the Rum War at sea, distasteful as it was, and it did a most creditable job considering the personnel and facilities which were placed at its disposal in comparison with the magnitude of the assignment and the problems involved.

Women Were Instrumental in Bringing About the Repeal of Prohibition

David Kyvig

In the following viewpoint, David Kyvig explains the role played by women in opposing the Eighteenth Amendment. It had been assumed that women favored Prohibition, as many did at the time the Eighteenth Amendment was adopted. But when its effects became apparent, many women were dismayed by the crime wave it caused and the fact that their children, seeing how common it was to drink illegally, were losing respect for the law. In 1929 the Women's Organization for National Prohibition Reform (WONPR) was formed, and it eventually grew into the largest of the anti-prohibition organizations and was influential in bringing about repeal. Kyvig is a professor emeritus at Northern Illinois University and an author.

SOURCE. David Kyvig, "Hard Times, Hopeful Times," *Repealing National Prohibition*. University of Chicago Press, 1979. Copyright © 1979 by University of Chicago Press. All rights reserved. Reproduced by permission.

One of the main pillars upholding the idea that the Eighteenth Amendment was unrepealable was the belief that American women, since 1920 fully enfranchised, could be counted upon to support prohibition nearly unanimously. Women had contributed mightily to the passage of the Eighteenth Amendment, with Frances Willard, Anna Gordon, Carry Nation, Ella Boole, and the Woman's Christian Temperance Union [WCTU] as prominent as any man or male organization in the dry campaign. Defense of the home, protection of the family, and concern for youth had often been cited as reasons for establishing prohibition and were expected to keep women firmly behind even an imperfect liquor ban. A decade of prohibition produced hardly any evidence to the contrary. The leading anti-prohibition groups remained almost entirely male, with only men listed as directors. . . . But in 1929 an independent and effective women's repeal organization, the Women's Organization for National Prohibition Reform, appeared to challenge old assumptions.

The spirit propelling this organization was Pauline Morton Sabin of New York. Not a campaigner for women's suffrage, Pauline Sabin seized the Nineteenth Amendment's opportunities with seldom-matched energy and effect. . . .

She was a delegate to the Republican conventions of 1924 and 1928, co-chaired Senator James Wadsworth's unsuccessful 1926 reelection campaign, and directed women's activities for the [Calvin] Coolidge and [Herbert] Hoover presidential campaigns in the East.

Pauline Sabin's concern over prohibition grew slowly. Initially she favored the Eighteenth Amendment, explaining later, "I felt I should approve of it because it would help my two sons. The word-pictures of the agitators carried me away. I thought a world without liquor would be a beautiful world."

Gradually, however, intertwined motherly and political concerns caused her to change her mind. Her first cautious public criticism of prohibition came in 1926 when she defended Wadsworth's opposition to the law. By 1928 she had become more outspoken. The hypocrisy of politicians who would support resolutions for stricter enforcement and half an hour later be drinking cocktails disturbed her. The ineffectiveness of the law, the apparent decline of temperate drinking, and the growing prestige of bootleggers troubled her even more. Mothers, she explained, had believed that prohibition would eliminate the temptation of drinking from their children's lives, but found instead that "children are growing up with a total lack of respect for the Constitution and for the law."

> "Mothers . . . had believed that prohibition would eliminate the temptation of drinking from their children's lives but found instead that 'children are growing up with a total lack of respect for the Constitution and for the law.'"

In later statements, she elaborated further on her objections to prohibition. With settlement workers reporting increasing drunkenness, she worried, "The young see the law broken at home and upon the street. Can we expect them to be lawful?" Mrs. Sabin complained to the House Judiciary Committee: "In preprohibition days, mothers had little fear in regard to the saloon as far as their children were concerned. A saloon-keeper's license was revoked if he were caught selling liquor to minors. Today in any speakeasy in the United States you can find boys and girls in their teens drinking liquor, and this situation has become so acute that the mothers of the country feel something must be done to protect their children." Finally, she opposed federal involvement in matters of personal conduct. National prohibition, in sum, seemed to Pauline Sabin to be undermining American youth, the orderly, law-observing habits of society, and the principles of personal liberty and decentralized government, all important elements in the world of this conservative, upper-class, politically active woman.

The Women's Organization for National Prohibition Reform was instrumental in bringing about the repeal of Prohibition. The organization released this popular poster in 1932 to promote its message that repeal would protect women and children—a reversal of a common theme used by the temperance movement. (© K.J. Historical/Corbis.)

She decided to found a women's repeal organization during a 1928 congressional hearing when Ella Boole, president of the WCTU, thundered, "I represent the women of America!" Sabin recalled remarking to herself, "Well, lady, here's one woman you don't represent." . . .

After publicly criticizing prohibition, Pauline Sabin nevertheless campaigned for Herbert Hoover. She was a party loyalist and believed that Hoover's campaign promise to appoint a prohibition study commission showed a receptivity to reform. Disillusioned by Hoover's inaugural address and planning to work for a change in the law, Sabin resigned from the Republican National Committee in order to be unhampered by party ties. Within a month, she denounced the Hoover administration for supporting national prohibition.

Founding of the WONPR

Pauline Sabin moved quickly to give form to her announced intention. . . . During the next two months three organizational meetings were held in New York, and Mrs. Sabin toured parts of the East and Middle West to seek support.

On May 28, 1929, 24 women from eleven states formally launched their endeavor at the fashionable Drake Hotel in Chicago. At an earlier meeting to select a name, the merely awkward Women's Organization for National Prohibition Reform (WONPR) won out over the truly dreadful Women's Legion for True Temperance. The Chicago gathering chose Mrs. Sabin chairman, formed a national advisory council of 125 women from twenty-six states, and reported organizing progress in several states. . . . The mere fact that such prominent women had met to oppose prohibition drew national press attention.

The WONPR opened a small office in New York. For a month or so, the AAPA [Association Against the Prohibition Amendment] paid the office expenses, but thereafter members' donations made the WONPR self-sufficient. Mrs. Sabin made speeches and wrote articles criticizing prohibition for producing more rather than less drinking, endangering youth, corrupting public officials, and breeding contempt for law and the Constitution. She struck a responsive chord, for in less than a year 100,000 members were enrolled and thirteen relatively autonomous state branches were formed. By its first convention, the WONPR had set its direction as a highly visible, non-partisan, mass-membership, volunteer organization. . . .

The Women's Organization for National Prohibition Reform's first national convention in Cleveland in April 1930 articulated a basic viewpoint regarding prohibition which would remain largely unchanged until the end of the repeal fight. Some elements of the women's critique of prohibition were peculiarly their own, while others were common throughout the organized repeal movement. The WONPR regarded itself as an advocate of temperance and believed that prohibition had reversed a trend toward moderation and restraint in the use of intoxicating beverages. WONPR spokeswomen expressed particular distress at the effects of national prohibition on children and family life. Temperate use of alcoholic beverages had been increasing up to 1918, maintained Mrs. Carroll Miller of Pittsburgh, one of the convention's principal speakers, "But suddenly true temperance was cast aside for a supposedly quick method of reform and Prohibition was inserted into our Constitution with the notion that people could be made better by legislative enactment rather than through precept, education, reason and persuasion." This flouting of the American belief in free will, she continued, had resulted in the law being ignored; crime, political corruption, and misuse of alcohol increasing; and a general disregard for all laws developing. "And because we women value the American home above everything else and because we wish the youth in that home to develop high character and to grow in uprightness toward decent citizenship," Mrs. Miller concluded, "we demand that these prohibition measures which hinder his development and growth, be repealed."

Advocating for Repeal

Time and time again, the WONPR expressed concern over the violence, corruption, and alcoholic excesses of prohibition, all of which, they emphasized, had a

Pauline Sabin is carried aloft by fellow members of the anti-Prohibition movement at an event in front of the US Capitol in Washington, DC, in 1932. (© Keystone-France/Gamma-Keystone via Getty Images.)

harmful influence upon American youth. The organization reprinted an article by a New York juvenile court judge blaming national prohibition for increases in child neglect and young people's disrespect for law. "Many of our members are young mothers—too young to remember the old saloon," Mrs. Sabin explained. "But they are working for repeal because they don't want their babies to grow up in the hip-flask, speakeasy atmosphere that has polluted their own youth." The need to protect children and the home became central themes for the women's anti-prohibition movement, just as they had been in the temperance crusade.

Also the WONPR shared AAPA distress at the apparent breakdown in the social fabric, the weakening of the ties between citizen and government which disdain for prohibition appeared to produce, and federal involvement in matters of individual behavior. The WONPR considered proposals calling merely for Volstead Act modification inadequate since, they argued, that would eliminate neither federal involvement in liquor control nor the criminal activity of bootlegging. The Cleveland convention unanimously declared:

1. We are convinced that National Prohibition is fundamentally wrong.

(a) Because it conflicts with the basic American principle of local home rule and destroys the balance established by the framers of our government, between powers delegated to the federal authority and those reserved to the sovereign states or to the people themselves.

(b) And because its attempt to impose total abstinence by national government fiat ignores the truth that no law will be respected or can be enforced unless supported by the moral sense and common conscience of the communities affected by it.

2. We are convinced that National Prohibition, wrong in principle, has been equally disastrous in consequences in the hypocrisy, the corruption, the tragic loss of life and the appalling increase of crime which have attended the abortive attempt to enforce it; in the shocking effect it has had upon the youth of the nation; in the impairment of constitutional guarantees of individual rights; in the weakening of the sense of solidarity between the citizen and the government which is the only sure basis of a country's strength.

The elderly presiding officer of the Cleveland convention, Mrs. Henry B. Joy, once a prohibitionist like her AAPA-director husband, summarized the broad sweep of the WONPR's opposition to prohibition. After noting increased crime, overcrowded prisons, social and economic distress, and loss of respect for law and the law enforcement system, she concluded, "To my view, the prohibition conditions constitute the greatest menace to our country's welfare which has existed in my lifetime."

The WONPR expanded even more rapidly after its Cleveland meeting. At the second annual convention in Washington in April 1931, Pauline Sabin announced total membership of 300,000 and "live, active organizations in thirty-three states." One year later, 600,000 members and forty-one state branches were claimed. By the 1932 election, membership reportedly had passed 1.1 million, and when repeal was achieved in December 1933, 1.5 million women belonged, it was said. Although membership claims are hard to verify and are probably somewhat exaggerated, on the basis of these figures the women's organization must be deemed by far the largest anti-prohibition association, three times the size of the AAPA at its peak. . . .

> The women's organization must be deemed by far the largest anti-prohibition association, three times the size of the [Association Against the Prohibition Amendment].

The WONPR's rapid and enormous growth, according to James Wadsworth, "made a lot of men wake up and realize that, 'By heavens, there is a chance of getting repeal if the women are going to join with us!'" Women prohibitionists, not surprisingly, were less pleased. One wrote to Pauline Sabin, "Every evening I get down on my knees and pray to God to damn your soul."

The WONPR assaulted the stereotype of total female support for prohibition in other ways. State branches distributed literature, lobbied legislators, studied liquor control systems, held public meetings and parades, and campaigned for repeal candidates or against prohibitionists. . . .

Why WONPR Won Support

Why was the WONPR so successful in attracting support and thereby shattering the image of women as unswerving prohibitionists? Some observers suggested that many women enlisted to improve their social standing, to associate with and emulate the fashionable ladies who led the organization. To some degree, this may have been the case. Scarcely a description of Pauline Sabin was published which failed to mention her grace and delicate beauty, her fine taste in clothing, and her prominence in New York society. . . .

All too often, however, the efforts of American women have been dismissed as trivial whatever the motives or achievements involved. A common means of discounting women's serious activity has been to attribute it to a mere quest for domestic improvement or social advancement. The women's organization, although largely middle and upper class in composition, drew women of various backgrounds and not only socialites. A noticeably higher percentage of WONPR members were working women than was the case in the population as a whole. A number who took up the repeal issue were regularly involved in politics, while far more participated in charitable or other civic causes. It seems unlikely that such active women were persuaded to join simply to follow fashion. One New York WONPR officer suggested that the importance of the social standing of the organization's leaders lay in the encouragement it gave to concerned but cautious women. . . .

Substantive objections to prohibition appear to have weighed heavily on the minds of many who joined the Women's Organization for National Prohibition Reform. Published surveys of female anti-prohibitionists, although admittedly quite limited, show them sincerely concerned that prohibition was subverting youth, the home and family, the economy, and respect for all law. The decision of the WONPR to declare the mild goal of

"Reform" in its name, despite its commitment to full repeal, may have boosted membership somewhat, but the general outspokenness of the organization suggests that most women knew exactly what they were joining and accepted the WONPR platform. Serious opposition to national prohibition, rather than social climbing, seems to have been the principal reason that, beginning in 1929 and 1930, hundreds of thousands of women aligned themselves with the repeal movement.

President Roosevelt Proclaims the End of Prohibition

Franklin D. Roosevelt

On the day the Twenty-first Amendment was ratified, President Franklin D. Roosevelt issued the following proclamation announcing the repeal of Prohibition and appealing to citizens to regain respect for law and order. He urges them to buy liquor only from licensed dealers so that bootlegging can be stopped and enough revenue can be collected in liquor taxes to avoid imposing other forms of taxation. (This point was a major factor in the support for repeal during the Depression, when the government badly needed tax dollars.) He also points out that the Twenty-first Amendment gives the government power to prohibit the transportation of liquor into states that choose to remain dry. Finally, he urges the states not to authorize the return of saloons and citizens not to return to the evils of the pre-Prohibition era by drinking excessively. Roosevelt was the president of the United States from 1933 to 1945.

SOURCE. Franklin D. Roosevelt, "Proclamation 2065—Repeal of the Eighteenth Amendment," December 5, 1933.

*W*hereas the Congress of the United States in 2nd Session of the 72nd Congress, begun at Washington on the fifth day of December in the year one thousand nine hundred and thirty-two, adopted a resolution in the words and figures following: to wit—

JOINT RESOLUTION

Proposing an amendment to the Constitution of the United States.

"Resolved by the Senate and House of Representatives of the United States of America in Congress assembled (two-thirds of each House concurring therein), That the following article is hereby proposed as an amendment to the Constitution of the United States, which shall be valid to all intents and purposes as part of the Constitution when ratified by conventions in three-fourths of the several States:

ARTICLE

"Section 1. The eighteenth article of amendment to the Constitution of the United States is hereby repealed."

"Section 2. The transportation or importation into any State, Territory, or possession of the United States for delivery or use therein of intoxicating liquors, in violation of the laws thereof, is hereby prohibited."

"Section 3. This article shall be inoperative unless it shall have been ratified as an amendment to the Constitution by conventions in the several States, as provided in the Constitution, within seven years from the date of the submission hereof to the States by the Congress."

Whereas Section 217(a) of the Act of Congress entitled "An Act to encourage national industrial recovery, to foster competition, and to provide for the construction of certain useful public works, and for other purposes" approved June 16, 1933, provides as follows:

"Section 217(a) The President shall proclaim the date of

(1) the close of the first fiscal year ending June 30 of any year after the year 1933, during which the total receipts of the United States (excluding public-debt receipts) exceed its total expenditures (excluding public-debt expenditures other than those chargeable against such receipts), or

(2) the repeal of the eighteenth amendment to the Constitution, whichever is the earlier."

At midnight on the day of the repeal of Prohibition, August A. Busch, Sr. (center) and his two sons seal the first case of beer off the line at the Anheuser-Busch brewery in St. Louis, Missouri, for delivery to US president Franklin D. Roosevelt. (© AP Photo.)

Whereas it appears from a certificate issued December 5, 1933, by the Acting Secretary of State that official notices have been received in the Department of State that on the fifth day of December, 1933, Conventions in thirty-six States of the United States, constituting three-fourths of the whole number of the States had ratified the said repeal amendment;

> "I enjoin upon all citizens of the United States . . . to cooperate with the Government in its endeavor to restore greater respect for law and order."

Now, Therefore, I, Franklin D. Roosevelt, President of the United States of America pursuant to the provisions of Section 217(a) of the said Act of June 16, 1933, do hereby proclaim that the Eighteenth Amendment to the Constitution of the United States was repealed on the fifth day of December, 1933.

Furthermore, I enjoin upon all citizens of the United States and upon others resident within the jurisdiction thereof, to cooperate with the Government in its endeavor to restore greater respect for law and order, by confining such purchases of alcoholic beverages as they may make solely to those dealers or agencies which have been duly licensed by State or Federal license.

Observance of this request, which I make personally to every individual and every family in our Nation, will result in the consumption of alcoholic beverages which have passed Federal inspection, in the break-up and eventual destruction of the notoriously evil illicit liquor traffic, and in the payment of reasonable taxes for the support of the Government and thereby in the superseding of other forms of taxation.

I call specific attention to the authority given by the 21st Amendment to the Government to prohibit transportation or importation of intoxicating liquors into any State in violation of the laws of such State.

I ask the wholehearted cooperation of all our citizens to the end that this return of individual freedom shall

Roosevelt's Speech Triggered the Repeal of Prohibition

Although several large organizations had been working toward repeal of the Eighteenth Amendment for some time, the idea did not gain widespread public support until July 1932 when Franklin D. Roosevelt endorsed it in his acceptance speech as the presidential nominee of the Democratic Party. His remarks were brief, but because he was a popular candidate who won the election by a landslide, they turned the tide. This is what he said:

> I congratulate this convention for having had the courage fearlessly to write into its declaration of principles what an overwhelming majority here assembled really thinks about the Eighteenth Amendment. This convention wants repeal.

Your candidate wants repeal. And I am confident that the United States of America wants repeal.

Two years ago the platform on which I ran for Governor the second time contained substantially the same provision. The overwhelming sentiment of the people of my State, as shown by the vote of that year, extends, I know, to the people of many of the other States. I say to you now that from this date on, the Eighteenth Amendment is doomed.

SOURCE: *"Roosevelt's Nomination Address, 1932,"* The Public Papers and Addresses of Franklin D. Roosevelt, *vol. 1, 1928–1932. New York: Random House, 1938, p. 647.*

not be accompanied by the repugnant conditions that obtained prior to the adoption of the 18th Amendment and those that have existed since its adoption. Failure to do this honestly and courageously will be a living reproach to us all.

I ask especially that no State shall by law or otherwise authorize the return of the saloon either in its old form or in some modern guise.

The policy of the Government will be to see to it that the Social and political evils that have existed in the pre-prohibition era shall not be revived nor permitted again to exist. We must remove forever from our midst the menace of the bootlegger and such others as would profit at the expense of good government, law and order.

I trust in the good sense of the American people that they will not bring upon themselves the curse of excessive use of intoxicating liquors, to the detriment of health, morals and social integrity.

The objective we seek through a national policy is the education of every citizen toward a greater temperance throughout the Nation.

In Witness Whereof, I have hereunto set my hand and caused the seal of the United States to be affixed.

CHAPTER 2

Controversies Surrounding Prohibition

The Liquor Business Is an Evil That Must Be Eradicated

Earl H. Haydock

Photo on previous page: A tin tray depicts the three little pigs enjoying a beer while prohibitionist congressman Andrew J. Volstead, as the big bad wolf, threatens them. The anti-Prohibition movement used novelty items such as this one to promote its cause. (© David J. & Janice L. Frent Collection/ Corbis.)

The following viewpoint is part of the winning speech in the 1914 National Prohibition Oratorical Contest of the Intercollegiate Prohibition Association, in which college students from throughout the nation competed each year. Earl H. Haydock argues that the liquor business is a social evil responsible for much human misery and that it must be eradicated. Voters have had a chance to abolish the industry every election since 1872 (the first national election in which the Prohibition Party ran candidates) but have not done so because the major political parties have ignored the issue. Many people have spoken out against liquor, but the only effective weapon against it is the ballot. He exhorts adults to use their right of suffrage and urges college students (who at that time were too young to vote) to assume moral leadership in order to free the United States from the plague of legalized traffic in alcohol.

SOURCE. Earl H. Haydock, "Our National Parasite," *Winning Orations in the National Contests of the Intercollegiate Prohibition Association*, ed. Harry S. Warner. Intercollegiate Prohibition Association, 1915, pp. 14–18.

Haydock was a senior at the University of Southern California and president of the class of 1914.

Has our republic any institutions selfishly blocking progress and sapping our vitality? He is indeed blind who would answer no. Fastened upon our body politic is a menace threatening our very life. The most potent cause of sin, sorrow, and misery in our land today is the legalized liquor traffic.

> The most potent cause of sin, sorrow, and misery in our land today is the legalized liquor traffic.

Must not every thoughtful person acknowledge its importance? We are confronted on every side by its powerful hand. We encounter it in every phase of national life. It is a social question because society has made it so! It is an economic question because enormous wealth has made it so! It is a political question because our Government has made it so! And it is a moral question because God has made it so! It is not only an economic, social, political and moral *question*—it is that, and more than that. It is as [Abraham] Lincoln has said, "one of the greatest . . . of *evils* among mankind." It is more than a *question* to be solved; it is a *curse* to be removed; a *sin* to be eradicated; a *parasite* to be annihilated.

In 1865 Lincoln said, "After reconstruction, the next great question will be the overthrow of the liquor traffic." But since that time this parasite has been fastening its grip tighter and tighter upon the vitals of our democracy. From the time of Bacchus men have drunk to excess, but the evil has not always been an organized institution, legalized and nurtured by law. Only within the last fifty years has our Government become "The Silent Partner." Uncle Sam is now hand in hand with the brewers, and builds great storehouses for the free use of liquor. There is enough rum stored in the government warehouses to supply the total consumption for three years if there were not another drop distilled. We license and protect this parasite despite the fact that it is now universally condemned.

Reason has condemned it! Morality has condemned it! Science has condemned it! Society and social reform have condemned it! Three-fourths of our territory has banished it! Fourteen of our great commonwealths have outlawed it! Even our Supreme Court has judged it worthy of death! Yet in spite of all this, every year sees an increase in the manufacture and sale of this poison. This tyrant lives and flourishes, grinding up our grain, debauching our men and women, prostituting our children, polluting the blood of unborn generations, damning the souls of its victims, and hurling the nation headlong to imminent catastrophe.

It transforms the loving parent into the fiendish demon! It transforms the promising voting man into the worthless wretch! It transforms the beautiful pure girl into the pitiable maniac! It transforms the cool-headed captain of the Titanic into a reckless criminal! Go into the asylums, the jails, the streets of our cities, the cafés, the dens of vice, yea, even into our homes, and we find the blight of its sting!

Liquor Must Be Banned by Vote

Why do we allow such a menace to exist? Why do we stand idly by and see it grow larger and stronger when we could stop it? Every time we hold an election—county, state, or national—the opportunity is presented to strike. Every four years since 1872 the people have had a chance to end the whole nefarious business at one stroke. But because certain political parties come with their brass bands, their million-dollar campaigns, and their indulgence in personalities, we go to the polls and vote as our fathers have voted, for this party, and that man, instead of voting for right and for principle.

A cartoon by the Temperance Movement from about 1900 depicts the voters' choice for Prohibition as one that supports mothers and children over the interests of brewers. (© Fotosearch/Getty Images.)

What remedy do the parties offer? The Democratic Party almost a century old, the Republican a half century, the Socialist a quarter of a century, and lastly, the Progressive Party—four generations of parties—and not one word in their planks against the greatest evil in America! They offer absolutely *no* solution. At every national convention resolutions have been presented, and at all entirely ignored.

There is only one party that has dared to attack the real issue. For nearly a half-century the Prohibition Party "has been the highest and most perfect expression of the political demands of the people." Marvelous seems the prophetic vision with which she [the Party] has foreseen our present-day problems; admirable the progress of her constructive programs. . . .

First and always has she denounced the liquor traffic as the paramount evil, and advocated nation-wide prohibition as the only ultimate remedy. She has stooped to no compromise, and has given no quarter. She has consistently presented to the voters an opportunity to conquer this arch-enemy of man. Yet last November less than two per cent of the entire electorate voted with her against this foe. Why did this occur? Why are we so indifferent? Why do we not unite and manifest our sentiments against this sin by our votes? Do we realize that we hold in our hands the Deliverer? Do we realize also that we are morally responsible for our votes?

Men may cry out against this octopus in burning words; they may write scathing lines against it; they may spend their time, their money, and even their blood, in carrying on a ceaseless warfare—indeed they have been doing this very thing for years—but the only effective weapon, the only telling instrument, is the ballot.

The schools may educate our boys and girls to let alcohol alone; the Church may sound the evils of intemperance; the Government may try to regulate and control the traffic; the social worker may rescue a few victims from the abyss; but so long as rum is manufactured, it will be drunk. The only effectual way to eliminate the drunkard is to cease creating him; the only way to cease creating him is to kill the institution that makes him; the only instrument of death to this institution is the ballot. We, dear friends, have in our hands the power to rid our land of this devastating plague. It *was created by law*; it is *nurtured by law*; and it must be *destroyed by law*.

The rum traffic blocks the path of progress. The question cannot be evaded, it cannot be ignored, it must be settled. The time is now.

I appeal to you, men and women of this enlightened age, to consider these facts. I appeal to you, voters of this Christian land, to awaken to the peril, and use the God-given right of suffrage without delay. I appeal to you, young people of college, in the name of progress, to *lead* in this, the greatest service to mankind—*moral emancipation.*

The whole world is listening for the shout of victory. Let us fight with the ballot, until we finally triumph. Free our soil from this scourge by voting unitedly against it! Let the fallacy of license die. Be not blinded by compromise. No longer regulate and protect this parasite for the sake of revenue, but rise in the spirit of liberty—the spirit that gave birth to our native land, the spirit that saved her from disunion and slavery—rise, and ballot for principle. Let us make this a land where equal opportunity is the privilege of all, where the sovereign voter is morally free, and where the people and the government are one.

To Prohibit Alcohol by a Constitutional Amendment Would Be Wrong

Richard Bartholdt

During the congressional debate that led to the adoption of the Eighteenth Amendment, Richard Bartholdt presents ten reasons why he believes such an amendment would be wrong. Although drinking can lead to crime, most crimes are not caused by drunkenness, he says. Prohibition violates the liberty of the individual, and human nature cannot be altered by law. People would lose their respect for law and find ways to evade it. In any case, the US Constitution is not the proper place for police regulations. In addition, the economic effects of Prohibition would be disastrous, both in loss of jobs and loss of the revenue from liquor taxes. And it is not true that such an amendment would be chosen by the majority of voters, because the thirty-six states likely to ratify it contain only

SOURCE. Richard Bartholdt, "Ten Reasons Why Prohibition Is Wrong," *Congressional Record*, December 22, 1914.

a minority of the US population. Bartholdt was a US representative from Missouri.

The fundamental argument of the Prohibitionists is that the use of alcoholic beverages is the principal cause of vice, crime, insanity, and poverty, and the only right way of dealing with the matter, they say, is to prohibit, by stringent laws, the making and sale and consequently the use of such beverages.

I take distinct issue with both propositions. First, it is not true that crime, vice, poverty, and insanity are, in the great majority of cases, caused by drunkenness. Second, it is not true that Prohibition will prevent those evils. . . .

Permit me now to give the House ten reasons why, in my judgment, Prohibition is wrong. Many more might be cited, but I have formulated the following as the principal ones, to wit:

First.—Prohibition is a deathblow to the liberty of the individual because it prohibits what is not wrong in itself. No despot in history has ever dared to prohibit what is morally right, and the attempt to do so would have cost him his head. The exercise of rights which concern persons individually, and whose exercise does not injure the neighbor, is a basic condition of freedom which Prohibition violates. The right to eat and drink what we please is an inalienable human right of which even a majority cannot deprive us without at the same time robbing us of our liberty. But let us go to the bottom of this matter. It has ever been the aim of the friends of liberty to wrest the scepter of government from the hands of individual rulers and place it in the hands of the people. Since this has been achieved

> "The exercise of rights which concern persons individually, and whose exercise does not injure the neighbor, is a basic condition of freedom which Prohibition violates.

in America the problem of liberty was believed to have been solved for all time, for no one dreamed that the nation would ever need protection against its own will or would ever tyrannize over itself. The Prohibition movement teaches us, however, that such tyranny after all is possible under self-government by the majority misusing its political liberty or its right to govern for the purpose of restricting personal liberty. In other words, we are dealing in this case with what John Stuart Mill called "the tyranny of the majority," an evil against which the nation must protect itself if it desires to remain free; for individual liberty, the right of personal conduct, is an inalienable human right which should never be taken away either by majorities or by law or constitution. . . .

Second.—Prohibition runs counter to human nature because the taste and appetite of man cannot be regulated by law. Human laws are powerless against the laws of nature. Pass an enactment abolishing the law of gravity, then jump out of a ten-story window and see what will happen. You will be picked up in a shovel. But, say our opponents, we should at least remove the temptation which the saloon puts in our way. This is the silliest proposition of all, for if we endeavored to remove everything which might tempt man we would have to abolish gold and money, eatables and drinkables, and finally even woman, for all of these might become a source of temptation to man. . . .

> "A thousand ways will be found to evade the law, and the result will be a nation of lawbreakers."

Third.—Prohibition undermines manliness. Its premise is that men are children, who must be led in the leading strings of law. Our conception, however, is that a man should voluntarily do the right and avoid the wrong, and that an interference with his self-control in personal matters is slavery pure and simple. . . .

Prohibition Would Undermine the Law and the Constitution

Fourth.—Prohibition undermines respect for law. A thousand ways will be found to evade the law, and the result will be a nation of lawbreakers, a condition which must inevitably lead to lawlessness and anarchy. If the 82 per cent of our population who are moderate drinkers will satisfy their wants in spite of the law, then every thief will find justification in stealing, every burglar in robbery, and all other criminals in their evil deeds, and many will be encouraged to break the law who otherwise would have remained law-abiding citizens. May Heaven protect us against such a state of affairs!

> By incorporating in it mere police regulations our national constitution . . . will be perverted, defaced, and desecrated.

Fifth.—National Prohibition by constitutional amendment is unworthy of a great people. A constitution should be a bill of rights for the protection of life, liberty and property, and especially for the protection of the minority. By incorporating in it mere police regulations our national constitution, of which [British prime minister William] Gladstone said that it is "the greatest charter of liberty ever struck off by the mind of man," will be perverted, defaced, and desecrated.

Sixth.—National Prohibition means the complete subversion of the fundamental theories upon which our system of government rests. By the wise foresight of the fathers of the republic the police power was reserved to the separate states upon which the exclusive right to pass sumptuary laws was thus conferred. This sacred theory would be torn into shreds by conferring police powers on the national government. I say "sacred theory" because all state rights men up to this time have tenaciously adhered to it. A thing such as federal police power could not be reconciled with it.

The Lasting Impact of Prohibition on Constitutional Rights

The Eighteenth Amendment set a precedent for federal government control over citizens' lives that many considered a violation of their constitutional right to liberty. But that was not the only impact it had on constitutional rights. A more permanent effect was that it brought about reinterpretation of the Fourth and Fifth Amendment provisions concerning the rights of suspects.

The Fourth Amendment prohibits unreasonable searches and seizures, but it is up to the Supreme Court to decide what "unreasonable" means. It had previously been assumed to mean that searches could be conducted without warrants only when there was probable cause to believe a suspect had committed a felony, or when a lesser crime was committed in the presence of an officer who observed it. This restriction made it impossible to arrest people suspected of transporting liquor in automobiles. The chief justice of the Supreme Court at the time was former president William Howard Taft, who considered strict enforcement of the Volstead Act essential to suppression of the crime wave Prohibition had caused. In the landmark case *Carroll v. United States*, he altered the traditional interpretation of the law in such a way as to allow prohibition agents to search the cars of people merely reputed to be bootleggers. This relaxation of the rule requiring warrants still applies to searches of cars for other reasons.

An even more significant case was *Olmstead v. United States*, which involved government wiretapping. Roy Olmstead, a smuggler of Canadian liquor who was popularly viewed as a hero, challenged his arrest and conviction on the grounds that the evidence against him had been obtained by wiretapping, which was illegal in the state of Washington. In addition to the question of whether wiretapping without a warrant violated the Fourth Amendment's guarantee against unreasonable searches and the Fifth Amendment protection against self-incrimination, there was the broader issue of whether evidence obtained by unlawful acts of government agents was admissible in court. In a famous dissent, Justice Louis Brandeis wrote, "Experience should teach us to be most on our guard to protect liberty when the Government's purposes are beneficent." However, the zeal to enforce Prohibition overrode such considerations in the eyes of the court's majority, and its tolerance of illegal wiretapping set the stage for the controversy that surrounds warrantless wiretapping.

Prohibition Would Harm the Economy

Seventh.—Prohibition means the confiscation of property valued at a thousand million dollars, property which has been acquired strictly in accordance with state and federal law. Even if all the arguments of the Prohibitionists were true, it is inconceivable that a nation, whose sense of fair play is proverbial, could seriously permit the wanton destruction of such gigantic values. Do not forget that the bonds of the United States are based upon the wealth of the country, and that by the destruction of such values the security of the bonds must necessarily be impaired and their market value depreciated. . . .

Eighth.—Prohibition will take the bread from the mouths of hundreds of thousands of employees and workingmen, not only of those employed in the breweries and distilleries, but of coopers, blacksmiths, glass blowers, wagon builders, bricklayers, carpenters, and so forth. Indeed, there will not be a single trade which would escape the calamity. To those should be added all the small dealers and business men who are now patronized by these laboring men, and the damage will be felt even by banks, wholesalers, railroads, and farmers, especially those of our farmers who grow barley and hops. The inevitable result would be an economic panic unparalleled in our history, a panic dealing a terrific blow to the whole nation and the devastations of which would equal those of a civil war. . . .

Ninth.—Prohibition will cause a deficit in the national treasury of at least $280,000,000 a year, for this is the amount which the government now collects from beer, wine, and spirituous liquors, and which, by the way, far exceeds our total expenses for army and navy. It is a tax which every consumer, as [US president James] Garfield said as far back as 1880, pays voluntarily, because no one need pay it who does not wish to. It is, in other words, the voluntary contribution which the moderate drinkers of the country make to the national household.

Giant beer vats are removed from a brewery in Washington, DC, as it switches from producing beer to making ice cream during Prohibition. The negative effects on business and the economy were among the reasons cited by critics of anti-liquor legislation. (© Bettman/ Corbis.)

How, I ask, should this deficit be covered? It must be by direct taxes, of course; but we have just imposed a new corporation tax, a new income tax, and a war-revenue tax. Do you propose to pile an additional quarter of a billion on top of those? No political party would ever survive the attempt.

Tenth.—Prohibition does not prohibit, and for this assertion I beg to submit incontrovertible proof.

If the patent medicine of the moral uplifters were effectual, the consumption of whisky should have been reduced by at least 50 per cent, because half of the territory of the Union has been voted dry. But what are the figures? The truth is that the consumption has doubled; in fact, has increased much more rapidly than the population. Again, the greatest percentage of drunkenness is recorded in the Prohibition states, because the number of arrests for drunkenness was five to nine times greater in those states than, for instance, in liberal Wisconsin. This proves conclusively that you can vote a town dry, but you cannot vote a man dry. . . .

I trust, let me say in conclusion, that the vote on this proposition will not be regarded as merely a referendum. It is not; and when our friends the Prohibitionists say that Congress, in permitting the people to decide the question, would not have to pass on its merits they are telling us what is not true. In the first place, the people at large will have no chance to vote on the question at all, because the legislatures will decide it, and this fact alone puts a tremendous responsibility on our shoulders, and for this reason: To be ratified the amendment requires the votes of the legislatures of thirty-six states. But the thirty-six states which the crusaders are counting upon to vote affirmatively do not comprise a majority of the people, so that the twelve big states with a real majority would actually be dictated to by a minority, and in a matter which the great liberal states regard as vital. . . .

The only protection which we have in this instance against minority rule must be afforded by Congress. Moreover, the founders of the republic clearly intended Congress to exercise its mature judgment in the matter of amending the constitution or else they would not have provided for a two-thirds majority to be required for the passage of an amendment.

Prohibition Is Necessary During Wartime to Conserve Food and Labor

Charles Stelzle

In the following viewpoint, Charles Stelzle exhorts Americans to give up drinking in support of the US effort in World War I. It is wrong, he asserts, to waste grain when it is needed for the troops—the amount devoted to liquor in the United States would be enough to feed all the soldiers being sent to the front line. The labor of the thousands of men engaged in the manufacture, sale, and distribution of liquor is also wasted, and life is wasted because these men's lives are shortened by their occupations. Stelzle believes food shortages are likely to be a factor in fighting the war because many farmers have gone into the army or to munitions factories. Some nations believe their soldiers need a rum ration, but US soldiers are not allowed to drink, and they fight as well as anyone. People at home have no right to drink when the soldiers do not.

SOURCE. Charles Stelzle, *Why Prohibition!* New York: Doran, 1918, pp. 22–42.

Stelzle was a Presbyterian pastor nationally known for his support of the labor movement.

There never was a time when America so needed her sober senses as to-day—it is a time when selfishness must be subordinated to the great task of winning the war.

We are being told by those who have come from the Front that we in this country haven't begun to feel the pinch of the war. Except for an occasional parade or brass band, a flag raising, a Red Cross or Liberty Loan appeal or something of the sort, it doesn't look much like war in the home town. . . .

Most of us flatter ourselves that, if we have bought a fifty dollar Liberty Bond, we have made about all the sacrifice that the country has a right to ask of us.

But—once in a while, when the boys march down the street with flags flashing in the sunlight and drums throbbing, we get a tightening of the throat and there's a moment when the picture blurs. . . .

Meanwhile, some of the finest fellows in this country are freely giving themselves for service in the trenches and on the sea and we honour them because of their readiness to serve their country.

Probably millions of our boys will go to the Front before the war ends, to do their level best to stop the tide of red ruin and outrageous killing.

But there's one fact that stands out clear and sharp as we take a world-wide view of the war—namely, that we've got to reckon not only with "Kaiser Bill Hohenzollern" [Wilhelm II, Emperor of Germany] but with "Kaiser John Barleycorn" [a personification of alcohol].

Every great general in this war—every great strategist who has had the courage to face all the facts has pointed out the danger of drink.

[Prime minister of Britain] Lloyd George put it this way:

We are fighting Germany, Austria and drink, and as far as I can see, the greatest of the three deadly foes is drink.

Marshal Joffre [a French general] said:

Alcohol by diminishing the moral and material strength of the Army, is a crime against national defence in the face of the enemy. . . .

And so France, England and Russia have grappled with their arch-enemy—but he is putting up the biggest fight in his history, for he knows that if he loses out in this war, he will be played out forever. . . .

> Food, labor and life are the chief factors in winning the war—but the liquor men are wasting all three.

Waste of Food, Labor, and Life

Food, labor and life are the chief factors in winning the war—but the liquor men are wasting all three.

They are wasting food:

Last year in the United States the waste amounted to 7,000,000,000 pounds of foodstuffs—and they have no right to starve some men by making others drunk.

They are wasting labour:

About 300,000 men are engaged in the manufacture, sale and distribution of liquor—in breweries, saloons and restaurants as brewers, bartenders and waiters—at a time when every man is needed in some useful occupation to help win the war. The labour of these 300,000 men is worse than wasted—no possible good can come of it, but much harm is done. Nor does this take into account the many thousands who produce the materials that are used in making liquor.

They are wasting life:

A US government poster during World War I asks citizens to "waste nothing" because food is direly needed on the front lines. The vast resources of food needed during the war are among the reasons why some supported Prohibition. (© MPI/ Getty Images.)

Bartenders, brewery workers and waiters in saloons lose an average of six years of life on account of their occupations. If the 300,000 men who make and sell booze lose an average of six years of life, it makes a total of 1,800,000 years of life. The average man works about thirty years—so that the liquor traffic is using up the equivalent of 60,000 men in each generation—and this is too great a price for the nation to pay.

For these reasons—first, because of the waste of food; second, because of the waste of labour; third, because of the waste of life, we have a right to demand that the liquor business be abolished.

"Food will win the war" is the slogan of the Food Conservation Campaign—and it's probably true. If food will win the war, the liquor men who are food wasters are not only fighting against our country, but they will have to reckon with us if we should lose the war.

When the United States Senate's Committee on Agriculture was investigating the subject of foodstuffs, the liquor men denied that they consumed as much as the prohibitionists said they did—they declared that they used only one per cent of the grain.

All right—let's take them at their word:

One per cent of the grain will feed one per cent of the people. This means one million people—because there are 100,000,000 of us in this country.

We shall this year probably send 1,000,000 soldiers to France.

This means that the liquor men have been wasting enough grain to feed every last man who will go to the trenches!

Food Needed to Win the War

If food will win the war—as [head of the Food Administration Herbert] Hoover says—then the liquor men have a fearful responsibility resting upon them when they deliberately waste the food which would give life and strength to our soldiers.

We have been told that it is altogether possible that the last million bushels of grain will be the determining factor in winning the war. If this is true, then how can we permit the liquor business to waste enough foodstuffs to feed our entire Army at the Front?

At a time when conservation is the key-note of victory, it seems suicidal to permit the liquor men to waste sugar, molasses, grain, coal and railway service, when the boys at the Front and those who are standing behind them need the very best that this country affords in order to win the war.

We deny the right of our soldiers to drink liquor—what right then has the man who stays at home not only to drink all the booze he wants, but by doing so use the grain that should go into the soldiers' bread—the soldier who has gone to the Front to fight for the life of the boozer who remains at home? . . .

With the shifting of large numbers of farmers to the battlefields in France, and to the munition factories in cities where they are getting big wages, there are fewer men than ever engaged in raising wheat—to say nothing about other food products—and the chances are that there's going to be great difficulty in harvesting even the reduced crop of wheat that we shall raise this year.

The increase in the population of this country has been three times as great as the average increase in wheat production during the past ten years over the average production for the ten preceding years. We are failing to keep pace in wheat production with the normal increase of population. If this continues, it doesn't require an expert statistician to tell us where we are coming out. . . .

Dare we shirk a duty which is plainly ours especially in view of what our Allies have done—or what they are earnestly trying to do?

The liquor traffic is probably not so strongly entrenched here as it is in England and in some other countries, but it's going to be no easy fight to put "John Barleycorn" on the shelf—and keep him there. . . .

War Prohibition Is Essential

Wherever American Officers are in complete control at the Front, practical prohibition prevails among our soldiers.

We can trust our men with such leadership—our real problem is with the man who stays at home.

Will he take his part by living the sacrificial life—although it seems like a mighty small sacrifice to give up a cocktail or a glass of beer for the sake of helping to win the greatest war in the history of the world.

Those of us who remain behind may dig the biggest trench in the world—a trench that will stop the liquor traffic forever.

This is a war within a war—a battlefield right here at home, and it calls for fighters and martyrs—it's a question of whether we're big enough to stand the test.

If England and France have not accomplished all that they hoped in their prohibition program, this is no good reason why America should halt in putting through a policy which we know is imperative if the war is to be won soon.

Nor does it matter whether Englishmen and Frenchmen have a rum ration in their armies—we have a prohibition Army and a prohibition Navy and we're proud of both.

It's going to be demonstrated that our boys will put up as fine a fight against the enemy as any Army which depends upon liquor to give it spirit and strength—there's no doubt that our boys will give a good account of themselves in this particular. . . .

Professor Irving Fisher, of Yale University, said in a brief argument for war-time prohibition:

> Every reason for prohibition in times of peace is multiplied during war, and war removes or weakens almost every argument against it. These facts explain why so many thoughtful and conservative men who have hitherto been against prohibition advocate it now as a war measure.
>
> In times of peace the liquor interests argue that they greatly extend the farmers' market for grain, but the war has brought a world food crisis, short crops, devastation of wheat fields, destruction of grain by the submarines

and withdrawal of men from agriculture to battlefields and munition works.

America must feed Europe, yet we have been complacently eating up our own food stocks and therefore have not yet realised that for the first time in our history, we, too, are about to face food shortage. Only those closest to the facts like Mr. Hoover realise this fully. Hunger and food riots are possible unless heroic measures are applied. Consequently childhood is asked to forego its pleasures by planting a plot for the honour of the flag.

Prohibition, by keeping sober one or two hundred thousand men now incapacitated each day by drunkenness and by increasing the productive power of those who while not drunk, are slowed down by alcohol, would speed up production probably at least 10 per cent. It follows that the more than two billions now spent on alcohol and the more than two billions of national income which prohibition would bring, could all be paid in taxes without making the people one cent poorer.

For the life, health and efficiency of the men in the military, industrial and agricultural arms of the national service, for the conservation of foodstuffs and for the soundness of our fiscal policy, we need war prohibition.

America practically holds in her hands the future of the liquor traffic throughout the world. What she does with her foodstuffs may determine the destiny of the liquor business in the countries of our Allies. They are watching our action with intense interest.

Have we the courage to destroy the enemy within our gates, who is stealing away our brains, weakening our brawn, and making flabby the morale of our nation at a time when all forward-looking men should be fighting to "make the world safe for democracy"?

Prohibition Is an Unjustifiable Violation of Personal Liberty

Fabian Franklin

In the following viewpoint, Fabian Franklin declares that Prohibition is an outrageous violation of individual liberty and this is why the law is so widely violated. Whereas all government involves some surrender of liberty, this surrender is justified only when restriction of a person's actions is necessary to protect the rights of others—it is wrong to restrict anyone's freedom on the grounds that other people believe it is for his or her own good. Franklin asserts that the resistance to the law is a good thing because if people had calmly accepted it, that would have encouraged more attacks on freedom in the future. Franklin was associate editor of the *New York Evening Post* and during World War I he founded a periodical called *The Review*.

SOURCE. Fabian Franklin, *What Prohibition Has Done to America.* New York: Harcourt Brace, 1922, pp. 97–106.

The tree of liberty is less flourishing to-day than it was fifty or a hundred years ago; its leaves are not so green, and it is not so much the object of universal admiration and affection. But its roots are deep down in the soil; and it supplies a need of mankind too fundamental, feeds an aspiration too closely linked with all that elevates and enriches human nature, to permit of its being permanently neglected or allowed to fall into decay. . . .

> The Prohibition law is so light-heartedly violated by all sorts and conditions of men . . . [because] the law is a gross outrage upon personal liberty.

The mass of the people—and I mean great as well as small, cultured and wealthy as well as ignorant and poor—retain their instinctive attachment to the idea of liberty. It is chiefly in a small, but extremely prominent and influential, body of over-sophisticated people—specialists of one kind or another—that the principle of liberty has fallen into the disrepute to which I have referred. The prime reason why the Prohibition law is so light-heartedly violated by all sorts and conditions of men, why it is held in contempt by hundreds of thousands of our best and most respected citizens, is that the law is a gross outrage upon personal liberty. Many, indeed, would commit the violation as a mere matter of self-indulgence; but it is absurd to suppose that this would be done, as it is done, by thousands of persons of the highest type of character and citizenship. These people are sustained by the consciousness that, though their conduct may be open to criticism, it at least has the justification of being a revolt against a law—a law unrepealable by any ordinary process—that strikes at the foundations of liberty.

Restriction of Liberty Is Justified Only to Protect the Rights of Others

Defenders of Prohibition seek to do away with the objection to it as an invasion of personal liberty by pointing

Two men smuggling rum across the Mexico-Texas border are searched. Constitutional rights regarding physical searches were substantially altered during Prohibition. Precedents set by the US Supreme Court in defense of the Eighteenth Amendment continue to impact the life of US citizens well beyond alcohol consumption. (© Underwood & Underwood/Corbis.)

out that all submission to civil government is in the nature of a surrender of personal liberty. . . .

Submission to an orderly government does, of course, involve the surrender of one's personal freedom in countless directions. But speaking broadly, such surrender is exacted, under what are generally known as "free institutions," only to the extent to which the right of one man to do as he pleases has to be restricted in order to secure the elementary rights of other men from violation, or to preserve conditions that are essential to the general welfare. If A steals, he steals from B; if he murders, he kills B; if he commits arson, he sets fire to B's house. If a man makes a loud noise in the street, he disturbs the quiet of hundreds of his fellow citizens, and may make life quite unendurable to them. There are complexities into which I cannot enter in such matters as Sunday closing and kindred regulations; but upon examination it is easily enough seen that they fall in essence under the same principle—the principle of restraint upon one individual to prevent him from injuring not himself, but others.

> If the Eighteenth Amendment . . . [made] the *drinking* of liquor a crime, instead of the *manufacture and sale* . . . it could not have been passed.

A law punishing drunkenness, which is a public nuisance, comes under the head I have been speaking of; a law forbidding a man to drink for fear that he may become a drunkard does not. And in fact the prohibitionists themselves instinctively recognise the difference, and avoid, so far as they can offending the sense of liberty by so direct an attack upon it. It is safe to say that if the Eighteenth Amendment had undertaken to make the *drinking* of liquor a crime, instead of the *manufacture and sale of it*, it could not have been passed or come anywhere near being passed. There is hardly a Senator or a Representative that would not have recoiled from a proposal so palpably offensive to the instinct of liberty. Yet precisely this is the real object of the Eighteenth Amendment; its purpose—and, if enforced, its practical effect—is to make it permanently a crime against the national government for an American to drink a glass of beer or wine. The legislators, State and national, who enacted it knew this perfectly well; yet if the thing had been put into the Amendment in so many words, hardly a man of them would have cast his vote for it. . . .

People's Freedom Should Not Be Restricted on the Basis of What Others Think Is Good for Them

In addition to its being a regulation of individual conduct in a matter which is in its nature the individual's own concern, Prohibition differs in another essential respect from those restrictions upon liberty which form a legitimate and necessary part of the operation of civil government. To put a governmental ban upon all alcoholic drinks is to forbid the *use* of a thing in order to prevent its *abuse*. Of course there are fanatics who declare—and believe—that *all* indulgence in alcoholic drink, however moderate, is abuse; but to justify Prohibition on that ground would be to accept a doctrine even more dangerous to liberty. It is bad enough to justify the proscription of an innocent indulgence on the ground that there is danger of its being carried beyond the point of innocence; but it is far worse to forbid it on the ground that, however innocent and beneficial a moderate indulgence may seem to millions of people, it is not regarded as good for them by others. The only thing that lends dignity to the Prohibition cause is the undeniable fact that drunkenness is the source of a vast amount of evil and wretchedness; the position of those who declare that all objections must be waived in the presence of this paramount consideration is respectable, though in my judgment utterly wrong. But any man who justifies Prohibition on the ground that drinking is an evil, no matter how temperate, is either a man of narrow and stupid mind or is utterly blind to the value of

> To put a governmental ban upon all alcoholic drinks is to forbid the *use* of a thing in order to prevent its *abuse*.

human liberty. The ardent old-time Prohibitionist—the man who thinks, however mistakenly, that the abolition of intoxicating drinks means the salvation of mankind—counts the impairment of liberty as a small matter in comparison with his world-saving reform; this is a position from which one cannot withhold a certain measure of sympathy and respect. But to justify the sacrifice of liberty on the ground that the man who is deprived of it will be somewhat better off without it is to assume a position that is at once contemptible and in the highest degree dangerous. Contemptible, because it argues a total failure to understand what liberty means to mankind; dangerous, because there is no limit to the monstrosities of legislation which may flow from the acceptance of such a view. . . .

Rejecting, then, the preposterous notion of extreme fanatics—whether the fanatics of science or the fanatics of moral reform—we have in Prohibition a restraint upon the liberty of the individual which is designed not to protect the rights of other individuals or to serve the manifest requirements of civil government, but to prevent the individual from injuring himself by pursuing his own happiness in his own way; the case being further aggravated by the circumstance that in order to make this injury impossible he is denied even such access to the forbidden thing as would not—except in a sense that it is absurd to consider—be injurious. Now this may be benevolent despotism, but despotism it is; and the people that accustoms itself to the acceptance of such despotism, whether at the hands of a monarch, or an oligarchy, or a democracy, has abandoned the cause of liberty. For there is hardly any conceivable encroachment upon individual freedom which would be a more flagrant offense against that principle than is one that makes an iron-bound rule commanding a man to conform his personal habits to the judgment of his rulers as to what is best for him.

Prohibition Sets a Precedent for the Disregard of Liberty

I do not mean to assert that it necessarily follows that such encroachments will actually come thick and fast on the heels of Prohibition. Any specific proposal will, of course, be opposed by those who do not like it, and may have a much harder time than Prohibition to acquire the following necessary to bring about its adoption. But the resistance to it on specific grounds will lack the strength which it would derive from a profound respect for the general principle of liberty; whatever else may be said against it, it will be impossible to make good the objection that it sets an evil precedent of disregard for the claims of that principle. The Eighteenth Amendment is so gross an instance of such disregard that it can hardly be surpassed by anything that is at all likely to be proposed. And if the establishment of that precedent should fail actually to work so disastrous an injury to the cause of liberty, we must thank the wide-spread and impressive resistance that it has aroused. Had the people meekly bowed their heads to the yoke, the Prohibition Amendment would furnish unfailing inspiration and unstinted encouragement to every new attack upon personal liberty; as it is, we may be permitted to hope that its injury to our future as a free people will prove to be neither so profound nor so lasting as in its nature it is calculated to be.

The Restriction of Liberty Imposed by Prohibition Is Justified

Arthur Newsholme

In the following viewpoint from 1922, Arthur Newsholme discusses what he has seen of Prohibition in the United States and concludes that the majority of the people support it and will obey the law. He believes it has decreased poverty, sickness, and crime and does not agree that it resulted in less respect for law in general. In Newsholme's opinion, restriction of liberty is justified when it prevents something that is injurious to many, even when it is harmless to many others, and he is convinced that in a democratic society, nothing will be banned unless the majority believes that it is a great enough evil to warrant such restriction. Newsholme was the former chief medical officer of the local government board of England and a lecturer on public health at Johns Hopkins University in the United States.

SOURCE. Arthur Newsholme, *Prohibition in America: And Its Relation to the Problem of Public Control of Personal Conduct*. London, UK: P.S. King & Son, 1922, pp. 43–48, 60–62.

The conclusions seem to be justified that National Prohibition in the United States is the will of the majority of its people, that the vast majority are law-abiding people who intend to obey and enforce prohibition, that to the extent to which it has been enforced it has doubtless been a factor in causing decrease of poverty, crime, and sickness. It has also been associated with greatly increased expenditure in useful directions, thus enhancing national prosperity and efficiency. Hitherto, no reference has been made to the possible sinister influence of Prohibition on the moral fibre of the people, to the conceivable encouragement of the "Thou Shalt Not" spirit of intolerance, "the joy of persecuting one's fellowmen", which in the past has been behind various forms of political and religious persecution, and to the possibility that "prohibition cranks" may enter into crusades against other forms of enjoyment, such as smoking, or theatre going, or Sunday games, even although these differ from alcohol in that no widespread social injury can be ascribed to them. . . .

I confess that such fears appear to me fantastic. It may be confidently anticipated that the general public will never give a majority vote in favour of the abolition of a personal habit, unless this habit is associated with national evils of serious magnitude. In this confidence we may confine our attention to more general arguments against the principle of Alcoholic Prohibition.

It is asserted that "prohibition does not prohibit," and that law is thus brought into disrespect; that in large cities and elsewhere, if one "knows one's way about," it is easy (though expensive) to obtain a supply of liquor. Liquor thus obtained, furthermore, is often much more deleterious than the spirits openly sold in the past.

That, hitherto, prohibition, especially in cities in eastern States, has only been partially enforced is true; but the statement sometimes made that there has resulted from this a lowered respect for law in general, and that the value of the oath has sunk, cannot in my view be justified.

The enforcement of any law against a practice which only becomes reprehensible when the law is enacted, e.g. smuggling, or as in this case the sale of alcoholic drinks containing more than 0.5 per cent alcohol, provokes the adventurous spirit and the covetous desire for illicit gain. But . . . the same tendency holds for many infringements of laws which nevertheless it is universally agreed must be enforced. The law merely converts potential into actual law-breakers and perjurers. The partial failure to secure prohibition in some States in the first year after it became the law of the land is but a repetition of what has happened in respect to other laws for the control of prostitution, of robbery and violence, etc.

Stress is laid on the inequitable operation of prohibition. True, it is said, it diminishes the total consumption of alcohol; but it withdraws alcohol from the vast majority to whom its consumption gives pleasure and satisfaction and whom it cannot be shown to injure appreciably, while intensified harm is done to the minority who still surreptitiously obtain alcohol and to whom it is especially dangerous, owing to their tendency to inebriety. So far as the majority are concerned, this point merges into the consideration . . . as to the extent to which it is justifiable to deprive them of an enjoyment for the sake of others to whom this enjoyment is dangerous and injurious. As concerns the minority it may be that persistent drinkers in a few instances are being more seriously injured than in pre-prohibition days; but this is a small offset to the vast multitude of such persons who now compulsorily are abstainers.

Drinking Is a Serious Danger

The argument from analogy is brought into play. Railway travelling, in recent years automobiles still more, are a frequent cause of accident; but regulation not

The Controversy over Medicinal Alcohol

In the nineteenth century, alcohol was prescribed for a variety of ailments such as anemia, high blood pressure, heart disease, pneumonia, and tuberculosis as well as for stimulating digestion and increasing energy. By the time Prohibition went into effect, the medicinal value of alcohol was beginning to be questioned; delegates to the 1917 American Medical Association convention adopted a resolution declaring that the use of alcohol "as a tonic stimulant or for food has no scientific value" and that its use "as a therapeutic agent should be discouraged." However, many doctors continued to believe in it and the Volstead Act allowed physicians to prescribe up to a pint per person every ten days. The amount allocated to each pharmacy was strictly controlled; nevertheless, plenty of people who were not ill found obliging doctors willing to prescribe alcohol for a fee, and some drugstore owners got rich selling "medicinal" whiskey. Many supporters of Prohibition therefore believed that the provision allowing medical use was a loophole in the law that should be eliminated.

On the other hand, reputable physicians resented government interference in their practice, and a group of them sued for the right to prescribe as much alcohol as they saw fit. "A peculiarly exasperating feature of the Volstead Act is that in putting its restrictions upon the medical profession Congress is not only assuming to know more about what a patient needs than the physician, but is actually practicing medicine, and practicing it ignorantly and incompetently, making thousands of persons suffer needlessly," said a spokesman for this group. However, in 1926 the Supreme Court, by a narrow margin, ruled that the power to limit medicinal use of liquor was a legitimate part of the power to enforce Prohibition and that the right to practice medicine was subordinate to the police power of the state. This ruling set the precedent for the federal government's system of classifying certain drugs as "controlled substances," a system that affects doctors and pharmacists today.

prohibition is the remedy proposed. Many men are ruined on the Stock Exchange; many others suffer from cardiac irregularity and defective vision as the result of tobacco smoking; but there is, and can, I think, be no serious intention to stop speculation or smoking. On the other hand public gambling is prohibited, and the public approve this law. It is evident that each case must be decided on its merits. There can be no pedantic consistency in regulations affecting personal conduct; but we may confidently expect that in a democratically governed country, a majority will not be induced in substance to prohibit a habit which brings enjoyment to many, but which in other instances frequently leads to poverty and to disease and crime, unless the majority is convinced on adequate evidence that the evil is of such a magnitude as to justify the limitation of enjoyment of a large part of the population.

It has been said that while the above view may receive acceptance, we cannot be certain that public opinion (i.e. a majority of the population) favours prohibition; it has been asserted that the American population have been overwhelmed by floods of emotional literature, and inflammatory oratory; that furthermore a large section of the population are more anxious to "be in the swim" on any popular question, than to form a considered judgment on it; and that prohibition is therefore merely a popular hysterical aberration to which there will be awkward reactions. . . .

A more serious objection is that prohibition, as a remedy for alcoholism, is the social analogue to the empirical treatment of symptoms in medicine, and is not directed to the removal of the causes of excessive alcoholic indulgence. . . . In the chain of events or network of entanglements which leads to drunkenness, abstention from alcohol, compulsory if necessary, is the most direct step towards the prevention and cure of drunkenness; and that, although compulsory abstinence may not be the ideal remedy, it at least prevents the formation of drinking habits, and on behalf of the drunkard gives time and opportunity to bring into action the physical, social, and moral remedies for the complex condition, which expressed itself in drunkenness.

> Prohibition only becomes justifiable as a policy when it is clear that intemperance is an evil of serious national importance.

It may, at the same time, be agreed that moral suasion and individual initiative are healthier and more valuable motives to secure temperance than the enforcement of prohibition; and that prohibition only becomes justifiable as a policy when it is clear that intemperance is an evil of serious national importance, and that other measures for its prevention cannot be put into effect, or that these other measures can only have a very partial success, or that this success will only be secured after many years or even generations of suffering from alcoholism. It may, I think, be confidently asserted, that notwithstanding the present increased sobriety as compared with past generations, the amount of injury and suffering to innocent persons as well as to alcoholics themselves caused by alcoholism is still a serious national evil, and that there is no early likelihood of adequate amelioration of this evil, under present conditions of manufacture and sale of alcoholic drinks. This being so, is not the case complete for the enforcement of prohibition, if a majority of the people definitely and persistently demand prohibition, and when it becomes evident that prohibition can be enforced?

Compulsion Is Necessary to Good Government

There remains for consideration the relation of compulsion, with alcoholic prohibition as a specific type of compulsion, to the general problem of Good Government. This is a subject in which every social well-wisher and worker, and especially every public-health worker, is concerned. . . .

The justification of coercion in a particular direction, is that it is action based on recognition of the real value of humanity, and aimed at the increase of this value. It has necessary limitations, resulting from the unwillingness of minorities to be coerced; and this unwillingness has been very manifest in recent politics. In general, however, a law which has been enacted under popular government can be enforced. . . . A law which will not bear the test of enforcement stands self-condemned. Whether Prohibition will endure the test of enforcement

An undated poster against the repeal of Prohibition illustrates that drinking and driving don't mix. Public health consequences of alcohol consumption such as traffic accidents were a common argument for Prohibition. (© K.J. Historical/Corbis.)

in an increasing degree in every part of America remains to be seen. It will certainly be put to this test. My own view is that the American public will endorse the action already taken, insist on its continuance and extension, and that prohibition will remain in operation as the law of the land.

The above general considerations lead to the following fairly obvious conclusions:

1. Compulsion is a necessary element in government.

2. Success in government can only be permanent when government is with the consent of the governed, i.e. democratic.

3. Democratic government is government by majorities.

4. Majority government is practicable permanently, and can secure the general benefit of society, only if the welfare of the majority is given priority over personal liberty; if majority rule is accepted even when contrary to personal views; and if no large proportion of the population demand the privilege of disobeying laws which run counter to their own appetites or opinion.

5. In nearly all civilized communities there has been systematic and increasing intervention, not only in regard to freedom of contracts and the distribution of wealth, but also in matters which imply diminished freedom of action for the many in order to protect the few, e.g. in the limitation of hours of labour, in the war-time provisions against excessive rent, and in impediments to the sale of alcoholic drinks.

6. In all such matters, moral action voluntarily undertaken would be preferable to compulsory action. But moral suasion acts slowly. Meanwhile multitudes of innocent persons continue to suffer, and the community suffers in pocket and in efficiency.

This is the case for compulsion, and it is a good case. When such compulsion is proposed to be exercised it should, as a rule, fulfil the following conditions: (1) It should, of course, be with the consent of the majority of the people; (2) compulsion must be practicable; (3) it must not be of such a nature or to such an extent that it will cause greater difficulties or evils than the evil which it is proposed to overcome; on the contrary it should be of such a character that the enforcement of the law will be likely to convert a recalcitrant minority to its support.

Applying these considerations to the case of prohibition of the manufacture and sale of alcoholic drinks, America can afford to hear with complacency [writer] G.K. Chesterton's gibe: "Your country began with the Declaration of Independence and ends with prohibition." For Americans prohibition is not a habit of mind, but a means to secure liberation from a great slavery; and if the will of the people remains constant, then America will have successfully carried through the boldest and most momentous experiment in social reform which the world has known.

The Volstead Act Should Be Repealed

William Cabell Bruce

By 1924 a number of organizations began working toward the repeal or modification of Prohibition. For the first time since the passage of the Volstead Act, Congress considered the issue. In the following viewpoint, William Cabell Bruce argues that the Volstead Act harms the United States, it is not enforceable, and it should be repealed. There is nothing innately criminal about drinking liquor, he says; many people are able to do so without excess, and it is tyranny not to allow it. No federal law is required under the Eighteenth Amendment; in his opinion the Volstead Act should be repealed and enforcement left up to the states, which could choose whether or not to allow beer and wine. Then the resentment against the federal government would die down and there would be less lawlessness. Bruce was a US senator from Maryland and a Pulitzer Prize–winning author.

SOURCE. William Cabell Bruce, "Is the Nation Ready to Respect Prohibition Law?," *Congressional Digest*, October 1924.

The true remedy for the appalling spirit of lawlessness that has been aroused by national prohibition is not to make another extraordinary effort to enforce it, but frankly to face the facts and admit that absolute national prohibition is not enforceable at all.

The Eighteenth Amendment became a part of the Federal Constitution on January 16, 1919; and the Volstead Act was enacted on October 28, 1919. It is safe to say that no period in American history has ever been distinguished by such general demoralization and lawlessness as the period of four years which has followed the passage of that act. To thousands and hundreds of thousands of American citizens it has become an object simply of hatred and derision. The flow of drink underground at the present time is almost as steady and copious as it ever was above ground.

The Injury Caused by an Unenforceable Law

The injury which has been done by this state of things to the morals and manners of the American people defies exaggeration. For the first time in our history the most reputable and the most disreputable members of American society have been brought into the closest working relations.

And this situation is not more notorious than the utter lack of power of the Government to control it. I can recall the time, before the adoption of the eighteenth amendment, when it was a common saying that, even if the States and cities of the United States could not enforce their laws, the Federal Government was always

> The idea that it is a criminal thing . . . to make, sell, or use an intoxicating beverage is a purely artificial conception.

equal to the task of enforcing its laws; and, for all practical purposes, the statement was true; but it is true no longer.

And why is the Volstead Act unenforceable? It is because the idea that it is a criminal thing at all times and under all circumstances to make, sell, or use an intoxicating beverage is a purely artificial conception, at war with the fundamental facts of human existence, and untenable in the forum of sound human reasoning. That murder or theft or some other offense of the same deep

Andrew J. Volstead, a Republican member of the US House of Representatives from Minnesota, penned the Volstead Act of 1919 that prohibited the manufacture and sale of liquor. (© **Corbis.**)

120

dye is a criminal thing, we need no Volstead Act to tell us. Indeed, we did not need even the tables upon which the Ten Commandments were engraved to tell us that; but the criminality of drink under any and all conditions exists nowhere except in constitutions and statutes written by men incapable, from fanaticism or other causes, of seeing things as they truly are. Millions of men can drink from their earliest to their latest years without the slightest excess, and I am glad to say that I am one of them. To divest this vast host of human beings of the right, under proper public regulations, to drink in moderation because there are, and always will be, a great number of individuals who cannot drink in moderation, is in effect nothing but sheer tyranny.

Such an act is not only destructive of every rational theory of human liberty but is prompted by a totally false philosophy of life. As long as we do not injure ourselves or others, there is no reason why we should not satisfy our sensual cravings as freely as our moral or intellectual. The human body is not a vinegar cruet; an odious subject for cloistered chastisement and mortification merely. It is, to use the beautiful image of [poet Samuel Taylor] Coleridge, "a breathing house not built with hands;" instinct and radiant with warm sensations, desires, and appetites implanted in us by God Himself, with the intent that they should be fully indulged in every respect so long as not abused. In these truths are the real insurmountable obstacles to the effective enforcement of absolute national prohibition.

Control Liquor by State Laws, Not Federal Law

Manifestly the thing for the people of the United States to do is to extricate themselves from the bog in which they are now floundering and to get back to the solid highway that before the adoption of national prohibition was safely conducting them to higher and higher levels of temperance. There is not a man within the sound of my voice who cannot say from personal observation that prior to the event the inhabitants of the United States were becoming more and more temperate or, in other words, more and more civilized; for advancing civilization is but another term for increasing self-restraint. They were drinking, of course, as they had always been doing, but they were drinking less and less in saloons and clubs and more and more only in their own homes as a part of their meals.

To the saloon, I trust, we shall never revert. So far as I know, there is no desire on the part of any of us to revert to it; but better the open saloon than the secret means to which the American must now resort to obtain drink.

Let the Federal Government repeal the Volstead Act and permit the people of each of the 48 States of the Union to pursue any policy in regard to the sale or the use of liquor that they may choose to do, subject to the limitations of the Eighteenth Amendment as interpreted by the courts. Then if there should be any State in the Union that wished to permit its people the use of light wines and beer within those limitations, it could do so without denying to any other State the privilege of pursuing an opposite policy. Under such conditions the bitter resentment that is now felt toward the Federal Government, because of its exasperating interference with the exercise of human liberty in a perfectly legitimate sphere of human enjoyment, would die down; the appalling and widespread lawlessness that now exists would abate; and the confidence of the American citizen in the wisdom and justice of his Government would be reestablished.

The Volstead Act Should Be Revised to Permit the Sale of Beer and Wine

William S. Vare

Opponents of Prohibition—favoring repeal of the Eighteenth Amendment, but recognizing that there was little chance of this because repeal could be blocked by just thirteen states—promoted modification of the Volstead Act to permit the sale of beer and wine. This alteration would not require any change to the amendment; in 1926 a Senate committee held hearings on such proposals. The following is a portion of the testimony of William S. Vare, who speaks of the great harm being done by Prohibition and presents the advantages of revising it. He believes allowing beer and wine would satisfy the US public and that the ban on hard liquor could then be enforced. The Senate committee, however, was not convinced by this or other arguments and recommended that the law remain in force as originally written. Vare was a congressional representative from Pennsylvania.

SOURCE. William S. Vare, "Testimony Before Senate Committee on the Judiciary," April 1926.

National prohibition has been in effect for more than six years.

The experience over this period has demonstrated the failure of prohibition under the rigors of the unreasonable Volstead law and that the only practical proposal for the enforcement of the eighteenth amendment is the modification of the act of Congress so as to permit the sale of beer and light wines.

Sobriety and temperance, the undoubted purposes of prohibition legislation, have not been improved by the Volstead law, but on the contrary there has been a remarkable increase of drunkenness and a crime wave so general as to startle the country.

Demonstrators show their support for legalizing beer during a parade in 1923. Some anti-Prohibition protesters favored legalizing beer and wine, while keeping hard liquor illegal. (© **Archive Photos/Getty Images.**)

Deaths from acute alcoholism, unquestionably due almost entirely to the use of poisonous substitutes, have been growing in number by leaps and bounds.

The increased use of narcotics throughout the Nation has been likewise appalling.

Courts are congested with pending trial lists and the delays in bearings have become a jest to the criminal elements.

The financial losses to the country through the enforcement of prohibition have assumed proportions equaling those of the war times. Not only have huge revenues to the Government been swept away, but vast sums of money, both through direct appropriations and otherwise, have been expended in vain efforts to make the Volstead law a success. Even at this time, when the house owner or renter is vigorously objecting to heavy taxation, and Congress is seeking to reduce the Federal levies upon the public, the more militant drys are demanding the spending of even more staggering amounts to further experiment in prohibition under the Volstead law.

> Hypocrisy and deceit have taken the place of justice in our police administration and confidence in Government generally has been undermined.

The moral costs as well as the financial losses likewise must be considered. General violation of the Volstead law has shattered respect for other laws. Hypocrisy and deceit have taken the place of justice in our police administration and confidence in Government generally has been undermined.

A Change Is Needed

Common sense now demands a change. Reaction against the unpopular Volstead law is sweeping the country. All but the impractical militant dry champions now appear to realize that if the prohibition amendment is to be made the success intended, the enabling legislation must be changed, and more moderate means introduced.

The sale of beer and light wines would provide a practical solution of the present ills. It would reduce the rigors of unenforceable prohibition. It would wipe out the market for poisonous substitutes and provide the Government with the opportunity to carry the real purpose of the eighteenth amendment into effect.

It would not only remove the burdens of taxation now resting so heavily upon the working people, but would permit still further reductions in Government levies, through the introduction of revenues from the sales of beer and light wines. . . .

Modification of the Volstead law to permit the sale of beer and light wines is needed to protect the youth of our Nation. The dangers of the present hip-pocket flask among young girls and boys are recognized everywhere. In my home city, under former conditions, liquor sales to minors were prevented through rigid regulations. To-day the former barriers are removed. The passing of the whisky flask, with its customary poison, is the expected event at the usual social gathering of youth. Formerly respectable circles frowned at drinking among the adolescents. To-day it is the accepted custom only too frequently, and boys and girls regard it as only smart to show their open defiance of the law of the land. Formerly the young man who brought the bottle of whisky to a party of girls was ostracized. To-day he is regarded as akin to a hero.

> "Formerly the young man who brought the bottle of whisky to a party of girls was ostracized. To-day he is . . . a hero."

It should likewise be borne in mind that the first appropriation for prohibition enforcement was only $3,375,000. The direct costs of enforcement have already increased sevenfold in seven years. Senator [William H.] King recently estimated that the greater part of the time

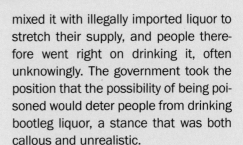

During Prohibition, Industrial Alcohol Was Intentionally Poisoned

Although Prohibition banned the manufacture of alcoholic beverages, alcohol has many important industrial uses that had to be allowed. The Volstead Act required producers of industrial alcohol to "denature" it by adding noxious substances that made it unfit for drinking. However, bootleggers soon developed ways of redistilling it to get rid of those substances, and some sold it more cheaply without even bothering to do so, as there were people whose desire to drink overrode any concern for health or unpleasant taste. The government, concerned over the large amount of industrial alcohol that was being diverted to bootlegging, then decided that it must be made still less attractive. Many poisonous chemicals were used, but the worst was methanol (wood alcohol), which has an odor and taste that was assumed to be an effective deterrent. Advocates claimed that government chemists were "not seeking to poison anyone, but only to render industrial alcohol unfit for beverage purposes by making it difficult to separate drinkable alcohol by illicit distillation. . . . The law requires a skull and bones label, to warn the person who might attempt to drink such liquor." Of course, bootleggers did not mark it with a skull and bones but mixed it with illegally imported liquor to stretch their supply, and people therefore went right on drinking it, often unknowingly. The government took the position that the possibility of being poisoned would deter people from drinking bootleg liquor, a stance that was both callous and unrealistic.

The situation first received publicity during the holiday season of 1926, when on one day, more than forty victims died in a single New York hospital. Thereafter, many warnings were issued, but the scare tactics did not work. During the next few years the national toll from poisoned alcohol exceeded ten thousand deaths, and an even greater number of drinkers suffered paralysis or blindness. While many citizens were outraged by the government's policy and it was hotly debated in Congress, some of the fanatic prohibitionists said that those harmed by it deserved no sympathy. They held that people who broke the law by buying liquor from bootleggers deserved what they got.

Methanol and other denaturants are still added to industrial alcohol in order to make it exempt from liquor taxes. But today, the availability of legal alcoholic beverages ensures that no one will try to drink the industrial varieties.

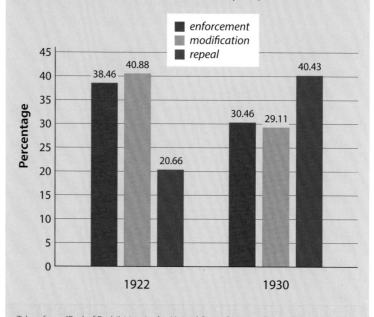

THE MAJORITY OF AMERICANS WANTED MODIFICATION OR REPEAL OF PROHIBITION

National polls taken by the magazine *Literary Digest* during Prohibition showed that the majority of Americans did not want the existing law to be enforced. In 1922 more than 60 percent wanted it to be either repealed of modified to allow beer and wine. By 1930 the support for enforcement had decreased further, and the percentage of people favoring repeal or modification had risen to nearly 70 percent.

Taken from: "End of Prohibition in the United States," *Literary Digest*, November 18, 1933. www.1920-30.com/prohibition/repeal-prohibition.html.

of 250,000 public officials of all kinds, with salaries of $5,000,000 a year, was being devoted to the enforcement of prohibition. . . .

Advantages of Permitting Beer and Wine

Modification of the Volstead Act to permit the sale of beer would restore an industry in which there was an investment of $792,914,000 prior to 1920. It would put to work in the beverage plants alone over 66,000 workers, including many thousands of others who would be employed in the making of boxes, crowns, labels, and the like. It would create a market for materials estimated at $123,685,489 annually. It would open the market for farm products which 13 years ago had a value of $87,520,287 or more than the total farm production of the States of Vermont, Rhode Island, and Delaware.

The advantages of the modification of the Volstead law have been splendidly summarized by Senator Walter Edge, of New Jersey, as follows:

> It would help make the Volstead Act honest by having it conform to the verdict of the country as alone expressed by the terms of the eighteenth amendment.
>
> It would decrease the demand for poisonous substitutes.
>
> It would minimize the domestic brewing and amateur wine-making industry, which has transformed many a home into breweries and distilleries.
>
> It would discourage the growing demand for strong liquor.
>
> It would produce a billion dollars annually and at the same time, by cutting down deceit, improve the morals of the country.
>
> It would contribute to contentment and thus greatly reduce the growing national scandal of law defiance.
>
> It would, after all is said and done, be giving the public only what they are always entitled to.
>
> It would not open saloons, but, on the contrary, and automatically close many illegal dives now practically unrestrained.
>
> It would salvage many a human derelict by providing a healthful beverage.

It would discourage the class distinction present conditions foment. . . .

Senator [Rice] Means: I want further to get your views. You believe also in the repeal of the eighteenth amendment, do you not?

Representative Vare: Well, I have not gone that far. . . .

Senator Means: You believe, then, that all that is necessary to be done to relieve this situation is the passage of the so-called Edge Act, which recites "intoxicating in fact"?

Representative Vare: I believe that would promote sobriety and temperance.

Senator Means: You believe that if Congress should do that, that these difficulties that you have referred to and these enormous figures which have, as you claim, polluted the life of America, would cease, and the remedy is all in this bill, is that what I understand?

Representative Vare: I certainly believe it would be going a long way toward effecting a remedy.

Senator Means: Then you believe that there would be no further call on the part of the people of America to repeal the eighteenth amendment?

Representative Vare: I am extremely hopeful that this would satisfy and create contentment of mind throughout the American people.

A Presidential Commission Opposes the Repeal of the Eighteenth Amendment

Henry W. Anderson

By 1931 a commission was established by President Herbert Hoover to study proposals for repealing the Eighteenth Amendment. It is known as the Wickersham Commission, named for its chairman. In its report, the commission described the serious problems caused by Prohibition, but recommended further attempts to enforce it, plus modification to make it more flexible rather than repeal. Henry W. Anderson, a member of the commission, agreed with the recommendation for modification but did not agree that Prohibition could be enforced, so he wrote a separate report, a portion of which follows. In the following viewpoint, Anderson considers enforcement impossible because the law violates the will of the people and represents an unwarranted intrusion by the government into the personal lives of citizens. Anderson opposes

SOURCE. Henry W. Anderson, "Separate Statement," *Report on the Enforcement of the Prohibition Laws of the United States.* National Commission on Law Observance and Enforcement, January 7, 1931.

repeat of the Eighteenth Amendment and the Volstead Act; instead he recommends that the government institute policies to carefully control the liquor industry. Anderson was an attorney and the leader of the Republican Party in Virginia.

T he facts stated and discussed in the report of the [Wickersham] Commission can lead only to one conclusion. The Eighteenth Amendment and the National Prohibition Act have not been and are not being observed. They have not been and are not being enforced. We have prohibition in law but not in fact. The abolition in law of the commercialized liquor traffic and the licensed saloon operated entirely for private profit was the greatest step forward ever taken in America looking to the control of that traffic. The saloon is gone forever. It belongs as completely to the past as the institution of human slavery.

> The saloon is gone forever. It belongs as completely to the past as the institution of human slavery.

On the other hand the effort to go further and to make the entire population of the United States total abstainers in disregard of the demand deeply rooted in the habits and customs of the people, ran counter to fundamental social and economic principles the operations of which are beyond the control of government.

As a result we are confronted by new evils of far-reaching and disturbing consequence. We are in grave danger of losing all that has been gained through the abolition of the legalized liquor traffic and the saloon. The fruitless efforts at enforcement are creating public disregard not only for this law but for all laws. Public corruption through the purchase of official protection for this illegal traffic is widespread and notorious. The courts are cluttered with prohibition cases to an extent which seriously affects the entire administration of justice. The prisons, State and National, are overflowing, but the number of lawbreakers still increases. The people are being poisoned with bad and unregulated liquor to the permanent detriment of the public health and the ultimate increase of dependency and crime. The illicit producer, the bootlegger and the speakeasy are reaping a rich harvest of profits, and are becoming daily more securely entrenched. The enormous revenues (estimated at from two to three billion dollars per annum) placed in the hands of the lawless and criminal elements of society through this illegal traffic are not only enabling them to carry on this business in defiance of the government, but to organize and develop other lines of criminal activity to an extent which threatens social and economic security. The country is growing restive under these conditions. The situation demands some definite and constructive relief.

The liquor question is obscuring thought, dominating public discussion, and excluding from consideration other matters of vital concern, to an extent far beyond its actual importance in our social and economic life. It must be solved or the social and political interests of our country may be seriously compromised. . . .

Social Causes of Existing Conditions

No law can be enforced unless it has the general support of the normally law abiding elements of the community.

The conception of natural or inherent rights of the individual as limitations upon the power of government and of majorities has been generally accepted in America since the Declaration of Independence. Whether this is sound it is useless to enquire. The existence of this conception is a stubborn fact of first magnitude. The distinction in principle between temperance and absolute prohibition by law is manifest. Public opinion is substantially unanimous in support of the abolition of the legalized saloon. But a large number of those who favor temperance and are unalterably opposed to the commercialized liquor traffic, including many who do not use alcoholic beverages in any way, regard the effort to enforce total abstinence by law upon the temperate and intemperate alike as unsound in principle and as an undue extension of governmental power over the personal conduct of the citizen. . . . This attitude of public opinion constitutes an insuperable obstacle to the observance and enforcement of the law.

Another fundamental cause for existing conditions is to be found in the character and structure of the Eighteenth Amendment. That Amendment is a rigid mandate controlling both Congress and the states. It is the first instance in our history in which the effort has been made by Constitutional provision to extend the police control of the federal government to every individual and every home in the United States. . . .

The cooperation of the several States was contemplated but the Amendment inevitably operated to defeat this expectation. It aroused the traditional jealousy of the States and the people thereof as the right of local self-government in matters affecting personal habits and conduct. . . . Many states are indifferent as to enforcement. Comparatively few are actively or effectively cooperating in the enforcement of the prohibition laws. In view of the statement of every Federal Director, or Commissioner of Prohibition, from the beginning, confirmed by the unanimous finding of this Commission, that the National Prohibition Act cannot be enforced without the cooperation of the states, this situation seems to require only a simple syllogism to demonstrate that this law cannot be enforced at all.

Even more important and controlling causes for the existing situation are to be found in the social, political and economic conditions to which the law is sought to be applied.

The Eighteenth Amendment and the National Prohibition Act undertake to establish one uniform rule of conduct as to alcoholic beverages for over one hundred

A Common Reaction to the Wickersham Report

President Herbert Hoover established the Wickersham Commission in 1929 to study proposals for repealing the Eighteenth Amendment. In 1931 the commission issued a report that described in detail the negative effects of Prohibition but nevertheless recommended further attempts to enforce it rather than repeal. Many people considered this an unrealistic assessment. Franklin P. Adams, a columnist for the *New York World*, summed up the report with this poem, which has since become famous:

> Prohibition is an awful flop.
> We like it.
> It can't stop what it's meant to stop.
> We like it.
> It's left a trail of graft and slime,
> It don't prohibit worth a dime,
> It's filled our land with vice and crime.
> Nevertheless, we're for it.

SOURCE: *Franklin P. Adams, "A Common Reaction to the Wickersham Report," New York World, 1931, p. 45. Reproduced by permission.*

and twenty million people throughout the territory of the United States. . . .

Some of the political divisions of the country have had centuries of existence with settled habits and fixed social customs. Others are but the recent outgrowths of frontier life and have all those characteristics of independence, and of resentments of social control, incident to pioneer conditions.

Few things are so stubborn and unyielding as habits and conceptions of personal or political conduct which have their roots in racial instincts or social traditions. As a consequence of this truth—so often ignored—the development of that social and institutional cohesion which is essential to the spirit and fact of nationality is always a matter of slow and painful evolution. It cannot be hurried by mandate of law. . . .

Experience indicates that if the effort is made to force this development by legal mandate the result is social discomfort and resentment, frequently finding expression in passive refusal to observe the law, or in resistance. If normal development is sought to be unduly limited or restrained it finds expression in social unrest or disorder and, if carried to its ultimate conclusion, in revolution. . . .

The social and economic outlook, habits and customs of the urban and industrial communities of the East are necessarily different from those of the agricultural communities of the South or West, of the more recently settled areas of the frontier. Those of different races and nationalities are still more widely divergent. . . .

These conditions are clearly reflected in the attitude of individuals and communities toward the observance and enforcement of the prohibition laws. Those who had been accustomed to use alcoholic beverages—who saw no harm in their moderate use and no reason why they should be denied this privilege—sought other sources of supply in disregard of the law. Public irritation and resentment developed. There was a revisal of sectionalism due to the feeling in urban and industrial communities that the law was an effort on the part of the agricultural sections to force their social ideals upon other sections to which those ideals were not adapted. On the other hand, there was, on the part of those communities which favored the law, resentment against those which resisted its enforcement. These things are not only prejudicial to the observance and enforcement of the prohibition law; they go much further, and affect adversely the normal operations of our entire national life.

Economic Causes of Existing Conditions

The economic conditions to which the Amendment and law are to be applied are of equally fundamental character and of even more conclusive significance. . . . Prior to the adoption of the Amendment, the people of the United States consumed more than two billion gallons of alcoholic liquors per annum. Neither the Amendment nor the law could eradicate this demand. . . .

Where a demand exists and that demand can be supplied at an adequate profit, the supply will reach the point of demand. . . . The operation of this economic law explains the failure of state regulation and state prohibition. . . .

The amount and quality [of liquor from domestic sources] are steadily rising and the prices falling. There is clear evidence that the drinking among some of the less prosperous classes of the population is increasing to a corresponding degree. Unless means are devised which will be far more effective than any yet employed or suggested to check this process it will inevitably continue, regardless of the present law, until the demand reaches the point of saturation approximating that which existed prior to the adoption of the Eighteenth Amendment.

It was the hope of many that with National Prohibition there would be a gradual decrease in the demand for alcoholic beverages until in a reasonable time it would substantially disappear. In the present study of the subject nothing has been discovered in past experience, or in operation of social and economic principles which would furnish any foundation for this hope. . . . The existence of an unregulated supply of alcoholic liquors at falling prices, the psychological appeal in gratifying a forbidden taste, the adventure of breaking a sumptuary law and the romance which surrounds the leaders of this illicit traffic, all have their profound effect, especially upon youth, and clearly indicate that the hope that there would be a decrease in demand was and is an illusion. . . .

The principles of economic law are fundamental. They cannot be resisted or ignored. Against their ultimate operation the mandates of laws and constitutions and the powers of government appear to be no more effective than the broom of [eleventh-century ruler] King Canute against the tides of the sea. . . .

Impossibility of Enforcing the Law

If the people provide a law of this character and then send into action for its enforcement, throughout the territory of the United States, a small field force of from 1,000 to 1,500 underpaid men against a lawless army running into tens of thousands, possessed of financial resources amounting to billions, ready to buy protection at any cost, the people must expect unsatisfactory results and heavy moral casualties. These conditions, to the extent that they have existed, have naturally tended to discredit the law. The same is true as to public killings, unwarranted searches and seizures, deaths from poisoned alcohol and other similar incidents of enforcement. There is a feeling on the part of many people, including earnest supporters of this law, that there must be some effective means of solving this problem which would not require the shooting of people upon the highways, the invasion of the sanctity of the home or the poisoning by the government of substances which are known to be used in beverages—especially where the purchase and use of such beverages is not even an offense against the law. These incidents of enforcement organization and method are deplorable. They have been contributing causes for the present state of irritation and resentment. I cannot find, however, that they have been or are fundamental or controlling factors in the larger situation. . . .

It might be within the physical powers of the federal government for a time to substantially enforce the Eighteenth Amendment and the National Prohibition Act. But under existing conditions this would require the creation of a field organization running high into the thousands, with courts, prosecuting agencies, prisons, and other institutions in proportion, and would demand expenditures and measures beyond the practical and political limitations of federal power. This would inevitably lead to social and political consequences more disastrous than the evils sought to be remedied. Even then the force of social and economic laws would ultimately prevail. These laws cannot be destroyed by governments, but often in the course of human history governments have been destroyed by them.

Upon a consideration of the facts presented in the report of the Commission, and of the causes herein discussed, I am compelled to find that the Eighteenth Amendment and the National Prohibition Act will not be observed, and cannot be enforced.

Repeal Would Be a Mistake

Many plans for meeting the existing situation have been suggested. They tend either to ignore essential limitations in our system of government, or are opposed to the lessons of experience, or violate fundamental social or economic principles. Only a few of the more important will be mentioned.

The proposal for the repeal of the Eighteenth Amendment, remitting the problem to the control of the several states, is strongly urged. I am unqualifiedly opposed to such repeal.

The repeal of the Amendment would immediately result in the restoration of the liquor traffic and the saloon as they existed at the time of the adoption of the Amendment in those states not having state prohibition laws. The return of the licensed saloon should not

US president Herbert Hoover established the Wickersham Commission in October 1929. The commission's report detailed widespread evasion of Prohibition and its negative effects on US society and recommended more aggressive and extensive law enforcement of anti-liquor laws. © (Keystone/Hulton Archive/Getty Images.)

be permitted anywhere in the United States under any conditions.

For fundamental reasons already discussed, state regulation and state prohibition substantially failed before the adoption of the Eighteenth Amendment. With further improvements in means of transportation and other social and economic changes which have since taken place, those measures would be even less effective today. I can see no sound reason for going back to systems which have already failed, and which afford no reasonable probability of future success.

As to the repeal of the National Prohibition Act [the Volstead Act], leaving the Amendment unchanged, the objections seem equally conclusive. This would be open nullification by Congress of a Constitutional provision. The repeal of the law would leave the Amendment without any provision for its enforcement. . . .

The proposal that the law be amended so as to permit the sale of light wine and beer is objectionable both on principle and from a practical standpoint. If the limit of alcoholic content were placed so low that the beverage sold would not be intoxicating in fact it would not satisfy the demand. If it were placed high enough to be intoxicating in fact, it would to that extent be nullification of the Amendment. . . .

I regret that I cannot concur in the view that further trial be made of the existing system before reaching a final conclusion as to its enforceability. . . .

I concur in the recommendation of the report that the Eighteenth Amendment be modified as therein stated. But the National Prohibition Act would still be in force. No substantial change in the Act, or substitute therefore, is suggested. We cannot stop there. . . .

A Proposed Plan of Liquor Control

The essential principles and requirements to which any plan of liquor control must conform may be briefly stated.

(a) It must preserve the benefits which have been gained through the abolition of the legalized liquor traffic and the saloon conducted solely for private profit.

(b) It must provide for the effective control and regulation of individual conduct with respect to the use of alcoholic liquors to the extent that such conduct is anti-social or injurious to others; but it must respect and protect freedom of individual action when that is not anti-social or injurious to the community. This will remove public irritation and resentment against the law, and will insure that support from the normally law-abiding elements of the community which is essential to its observance and effective enforcement.

(c) It must be sufficiently flexible to admit of ready adaptation to changing conditions and methods of evasion. . . .

(d) It must conform to the requirements of sound economic principles, and recognize the irresistible power of the law of supply and demand. It must take the profit out of every phase of the illegal traffic, and employ the force of economic law to defeat that traffic, instead of attempting to oppose the principles, permitting them to operate in favor of the law-breaker. . . .

(e) Finally, the profits of the liquor traffic should be used for the destruction of that traffic and the prevention of crime. . . .

It is proposed that as soon as practicable, by appropriate action of Congress and of the States, the Eighteenth Amendment be modified or revised, as recommended by the Commission, to read as follows:

> The Congress shall have power to regulate or to prohibit the manufacture, traffic in or transportation of intoxicating liquors within, the importation thereof into, and the exportation thereof from the United States and all territory subject to the jurisdiction thereof, for beverage purposes.

This modification would bring the Amendment into conformity with the traditional principles of our system of government. By conferring power upon Congress, it would give to the Amendment the necessary flexibility. The power to prohibit should be given to the end that if the proposed modification is adopted the National Prohibition Act would continue in force thereunder until Congress enacted some other plan, thus avoiding any break in the system of control and preventing the restoration of the saloon anywhere in the United States. . . .

We must not lose what has been gained by the abolition of the saloon. We can neither ignore the appalling conditions which this Commission has found to exist, and to be steadily growing worse, nor submit to their continuance. The time has arrived when in the interest of our country we should lay aside theories and emotions, free our minds from the blinding influence of prejudice and meet the problem as it exists. Forgetting those things which are behind we must bring into action against existing evils the great reserve of American common sense, guided by practical and successful experience. By this means, we shall advance the cause of temperance and achieve an effective solution of the liquor problem.

Prohibition Is the Cause of the United States' Continuing Economic Depression

San Antonio Light

In the following viewpoint, an editorialist for the *San Antonio Light* argues that Prohibition is the cause of the continuing economic depression, which began two years earlier. The consequences of poisonous bootlegged whiskey might be tolerable, the author says, but the nation cannot afford bootlegging when it takes a profit greater than the total revenue of the federal government. It cannot afford the millions spent to suppress liquor traffic. Moreover, Prohibition has caused an alarming use of whiskey in high schools and caused college students who previously did not drink excessively to start. Far from leading to morality, it has resulted in corruption of public officials and a crime wave. But because wets and drys hate each other, and have brought religion into the debate,

---

SOURCE. "They Wonder, We Do Not," *San Antonio Light*, April 5, 1931. Copyright © 1931 by Hearst Newspapers, LLC. All rights reserved. Reproduced by permission.

nothing is being done to take the profit out of bootlegging. *San Antonio Light* was a daily newspaper in San Antonio, Texas.

Depressions come and they go. But many of us would like to know something about the Cause. Why is it that we dropped from the height of prosperity, with not enough workmen, not enough factories, to a condition of unemployment, stagnation and factories shutdown?

Depressions or "slumps" are like the measles with children. All nations and all children have them. They recover and usually are none the worse.

But, if a child had measles for two years you would ask questions. With a slump lasting two years the people ask "What's the matter?"

Our European friends also ask "What's the matter?"

This picture [a cartoon showing Uncle Sam weighed down by a ball and chain labeled "bootlegging"] is one answer to the question, although it doesn't answer the whole question.

Our cousin, John Bull [generic term for a typical Englishman], and some of his neighbors are eager for a renewal of American loans.

They know that the United States has nearly five billion dollars in gold piled up, more gold than we need, that it has more than it can use of everything, oil, coal, sugar.

Why then does he sit inactive?

It puzzles Europe, but it need not puzzle us at home for we can see under the table, we know at least two of the things that are holding Uncle Sam and delaying recovery.

We live under prohibition, fastened upon the necks of the American people, an experiment heretofore untried nationally in this country, one that has failed and been abandoned in other countries that have tried it nationally.

Doubtless prohibitionists meant well. The sincere prohibitionist said to himself: "I don't drink. I am proud of myself. I am going to keep everybody else from drinking, and make everybody proud and happy."

The more or less hypocritical prohibitionist said: "I do drink. I wish I could stop. Perhaps prohibition would help me to stop, so let us have prohibition."

Now we have prohibition, we have bootlegging, we have the vilest imitation poisonous whiskey ever inflicted on a people, coerced into prohibition against their will.

> We cannot afford the bootlegging that actually takes as profit a revenue greater than the total revenue of the United States government.

We might say of those blinded by bootleg liquor: "It serves them right; they should not drink."

We might afford the deaths that have been caused by the Government deliberately poisoning alcohol. After all, one day's war would kill more than one year's whiskey. All by itself prohibition might be endurable.

The Nation Cannot Afford Bootlegging

But . . . we can't afford what goes with prohibition. It breeds bootlegging, and that in turn breeds crime on a scale hitherto unknown.

We cannot afford the bootlegging that actually takes as profit a revenue greater than the total revenue of the United States government.

If you learned that, without the knowledge of the people, the Government was spending harmfully more than its total legitimate income, what would you say? You would say "that explains our trouble, we can't spend billions for legitimate Government, and then spend even more billions on crime and survive."

Many billions, not merely millions, but thousands of millions, are contributed by the people of the United

Photo on following page: Unemployed and homeless men wait in line for food in New York City in 1932. During the Depression, millions of Americans were jobless, and some critics argued that Prohibition contributed greatly to the nation's economic problems.
(© Fotosearch/Getty Images.)

States every year to finance this country's gigantic army of bootleggers, and the criminal organizations that bootleggers have built up.

Crime has spread from bootlegging to racketeering, and to wholesale murder. It controls the baser types of public officials, magistrates, police. The corrupt element is kept on the bootleg-prohibition-crime payroll.

In New York a policeman, earning $2,500 a year, deposited more than $100,000 in his bank account in two years. Questioned about it, he replied "None of your business."

This picture shows the situation, as we see it, looking at things from our side of the ocean, observing the bootleg-crime ball and chain fastened to our Government.

We have seven million unemployed, according to the American Federation of Labor.

They represent the loss of spending power amounting to more than twenty million dollars a day, not counting profits that employers would make on the labor, were it at work.

We have organized bootlegging and crime taking five billion dollars a year from the United States people.

We have a government spending billions for its own expenses and paying off its war debts with unnecessary speed, with the best of intentions doubtless, possibly with a slight element of financial vanity.

Who will file these heavy chains and free the United States from prohibition, bootlegging and from bootleg-crime? The Government spends millions upon millions yearly to suppress the whiskey traffic and spends the money vainly. Bootleggers stand ready to put on their payroll at five and ten times Uncle Sam's salary those that he hires to enforce the law.

The most ardent prohibitionist cannot deny that this picture shows the situation as it is. Bootlegging costs more than the Government costs. Crime, bribing public officials, makes a mockery of justice.

The attempt to enforce prohibition, while preventing the use of mild and comparatively harmless stimulants, such as wine and beer, has made bootleg whiskey the national drink.

Prohibition Has Demoralized Youth

Prohibitionists said hopefully: "A young generation will grow up, that will know nothing of whiskey and have no interest in it."

The young generation *has* grown up and it carries a whiskey flask on its hip.

Public authorities are alarmed by the use of whiskey in high schools. Three of the greatest educators in the United States, Dr. Hibben, head of Princeton; Dr. Abbott, head of the Lawrenceville School, with five hundred young boys under his care; and Dr. Hopkins, president of Dartmouth College, all agree that prohibition, with its bootlegging, has demoralized youth, and caused excessive drinking among a class of young men that did not drink to excess before prohibition came in.

What they say is not theory. No prohibitionist can contradict them, or deny the truth of their statements.

They see the boys, they know what happens when those boys go home on their vacations. They know how it affects the young to see their fathers and mothers openly breaking the law, and laughing at it, talking of their "excellent bootleggers." . . .

> Prohibition . . . has made drunkards of many young people, and has made hypocrites of thousands.

Prohibition, far from stopping the use of alcohol, has made drunkards of many young people, and has made hypocrites of thousands.

The problem of prohibition, that has taken hundreds of millions of legitimate income from the Government and compelled it to spend millions in vain, is one of the most serious problems in this day of depression.

No one would suggest exchanging morality or good conduct for profit or prosperity.

But the trouble is that, with prohibition, you don't get morality or good conduct. You get corrupt officials, corrupt magistrates, and prohibition officials, notoriously bribed. And with the flood of bootleg whiskey you get a flood of crime that has been equaled in no other country on earth.

American citizens should discuss their problem temperately, sincerely.

Unfortunately wets hate drys and drys hate wets. And the question of religion, which should never enter politics, has entered into discussions of wets and drys.

The facts are that we have a gigantic crime wave which will last while bootlegging is able to finance it to the extent of millions a year.

We live in a bootleg-whiskey era which undoubtedly will last as long as prohibition makes bootlegging profitable.

What do the people intend to do about it?

Today's War on Drugs Has Created the Same Problems That the Prohibition of Alcohol Did

Norm Stamper

In the following viewpoint, Norm Stamper argues that the prohibition of alcohol made it valuable to criminals and led to the rise of crime syndicates, yet did little to discourage drinking. Moreover, it undermined respect for authority, especially among young people, just as is occurring today. Drug war violence today is even worse than the violence that arose under alcohol prohibition. Legalizing alcohol eliminated the profit in the criminal sale of it and the associated violence. In Stamper's opinion legalizing drugs would have the same effect. Stamper is a police veteran and a speaker for Law Enforcement Against Prohibition (LEAP).

SOURCE. Norm Stamper, "Prohibition: A Parallel to Modern War on Drugs," *Seattle Times*, September 30, 2011. Copyright © 2011 by the Seattle Times. All rights reserved. Reproduced by permission.

Ken Burns' new documentary on alcohol prohibition, premiering on PBS Sunday [October 2, 2011], reportedly begins with a Mark Twain quote: "It is the prohibition that makes anything precious."

As a retired police officer who worked to enforce today's prohibition—the "war on drugs"—I think it's a lesson we would do well to remember.

It was the prohibition of alcohol that made it so valuable to criminals, providing the tax-free dollars that turned neighborhood street gangs into national crime syndicates headed by the likes of Al Capone and Charles ("Lucky") Luciano.

Prohibition did little to curb liquor consumption, particularly among young people. Moreover, as otherwise law-abiding citizens were suddenly deemed criminals, the resulting hypocrisy significantly undermined respect for authority.

Today, drug use, especially by adolescents, is shockingly widespread, and law enforcement's job has been made that much harder. In cities across the country, young people, poor people and people of color have come to view us as the enemy.

Our drug laws have given rise to a new generation of gangsters with names like Sinaloa, Los Zetas and La Familia. These evil and greedy cartels are raking in profits that Capone and his ilk could only have dreamed of.

Unprecedented Violence

Like the bootleggers of old, today's international cartels reap untold billions of dollars from the drug war, and they aren't afraid to kill to protect profits or expand markets. After alcohol prohibition took effect, the homicide rate skyrocketed by 78 percent. Nearly a century later, 4,323 U.S. homicides between 2005 and 2009 have been directly traced to the illegal drug trade—more than the number of Americans killed on 9/11 or in combat in Iraq. Even this figure pales in comparison to the 40,000

Some Believe It Is Time to Revive WONPR

The original Women's Organization for National Prohibition Reform (WONPR), founded in 1929, worked to bring about the repeal of alcohol prohibition on the grounds that it was causing harm to society, especially to families and children. It disbanded in 1933 once that goal was achieved. However, in 2004 WONPR was revived by a small group of women who, like many others, believe that the current war on drugs is causing the same kinds of harm. On its website, the organization states:

> After thirty years of a failed "War on Drugs," the tragic consequences of prohibition are back—gang warfare, arbitrary and racially biased enforcement, corrupt politicians, and broken homes. It is clear that the drug war is a war on families, children, women, minorities, the poor and the disenfranchised. . . . As the life-bearers of this planet, we have a duty to protect and defend the children. It is our responsibility as women to learn the facts on this issue, to share our knowledge and begin to raise awareness of the crimes our system is committing.

murders in Mexico since 2006 that are directly related to the illegal drug market.

It would be difficult for anyone who lived under alcohol prohibition to imagine today's drug war-related violence. Whereas the St. Valentine's Day massacre of seven alcohol-trafficking gangsters in Chicago made international headlines in 1929, today's drug cartels regularly kidnap and murder police and other government officials, roll severed heads into nightclubs and hang mutilated bodies from bridges—complete with threatening messages carved into the flesh. The violence is so frequent that each grisly incident is but a blip on the radar.

Just as in the 1920s, this violence stems from disputes over territory. Instead of bringing whiskey from Canada, organized criminals deliver illegal drugs from Mexico via a sophisticated network whose tentacles extend from our southwestern border to more than 1,000 American cities.

Previews show that Burns' documentary vividly depicts the lavish lifestyles of Prohibition-era gangsters, the more successful of whom banked staggering profits for their time.

Yet today's drug cartels are even more profitable. It costs about $75 to produce a pound of marijuana,

In 2009 in Tucson, Arizona, a US border patrol agent and a Pima County officer search a drug smuggler's vehicle transporting marijuana into the United States from Mexico. Some law enforcement professionals believe that the war on drugs does not benefit society. (© Matt Nager/ Bloomberg via Getty Images.)

which then sells for about $6,000, depending on quality. Mexico alone produces more than 5,000 metric tons yearly, according to the U.S. Justice Department.

As with every historical documentary, we all know the ending to this one: At long last, Americans of all political stripes realized that the Prohibition experiment was a complete failure. Support for it collapsed, and repeal finally came with the 21st Amendment in 1933.

> Legalizing alcohol shut off a major source of funding for organized crime and took the violence out of the market.

The repeal allowed the creation of thousands of new jobs in a reinvigorated alcohol industry, with millions of dollars earned in tax revenues.

Legalizing alcohol shut off a major source of funding for organized crime and took the violence out of the market. It's not surprising that you haven't seen any newspaper headlines recently about Budweiser and Coors distributors shooting one another over who gets to stock liquor stores.

It took just 13 years for the country to come to its senses. But our drug laws have been on the books for decades. Nevertheless, I believe we are closer than ever to undoing some of the damage through current initiatives to legalize marijuana.

With so many parallels to the past in evidence, Burns' latest work should touch off a long-overdue discussion about ending our current experiment with the war on drugs.

Today's War on Drugs Is Not Comparable to the Failure of Alcohol Prohibition

Kevin A. Sabet

In the following viewpoint, Kevin A. Sabet argues that the United States' experience with Prohibition is not comparable to the illegality of drugs because during Prohibition personal use of alcohol was not illegal, the law was not strictly enforced, and alcohol has a long history of accepted use, whereas drugs do not. Furthermore, in his opinion the prohibition of alcohol was not a total failure and organized crime actually began prior to Prohibition. He believes that when a substance is legal and prices are low, there are heavy social costs, and he does not think that the benefits of drug legalization would outweigh those costs. Sabet is a former senior policy advisor to President Barack Obama's drug czar and is currently a consultant at the Center for Substance Abuse Solutions at the University of Pennsylvania.

Prohibition—America's notoriously "failed social experiment" to rid the country of alcohol—took center stage this week [October 2, 2011] as PBS broadcast Ken Burns' highly acclaimed series on the subject. And already, it has been seized on by drug legalization advocates, who say it proves that drug prohibition should be abandoned.

But a closer look at what resulted from alcohol prohibition and its relevance to today's anti-drug effort reveals a far more nuanced picture than the legalization lobby might like to admit.

As argued by Harvard's Mark Moore and other astute policy observers, alcohol prohibition had beneficial effects along with the negative ones. Alcohol use plummeted among the general population. Cirrhosis of the liver fell by 66% among men. Arrests for public drunkenness declined by half.

Yes, organized crime was emboldened, but the mob was already powerful before Prohibition, and it continued to be long after.

No one is suggesting that alcohol prohibition should be reinstated. Americans have concluded that the right to drink outweighs public health and safety consequences. But it is important to remember that the policy was not the complete failure that most think it was, and so we should be wary of misapplying its lessons.

If our experience with Prohibition was a nuanced one, then it is surely a stretch to apply the so-called conventional wisdom associated with it to help us shape policies on other intoxicants today. Still, a favorite argument of drug legalization supporters is that because "we all know" alcohol prohibition failed, drug prohibition is destined to fail too. Given modern America's thirst for liquor, it is a clever political maneuver to link the

> There are key differences between [Prohibition] and modern-day drug enforcement that render a comparison almost useless for serious policy analysis.

two policies in this way. But notwithstanding one's position on the success or failure of alcohol prohibition, there are key differences between that policy and modern-day drug enforcement that render a comparison almost useless for serious policy analysis.

Differences Between Prohibition and the War on Drugs

First, it should be remembered that unlike illegal drugs today, alcohol was never prohibited altogether. Laws forbade the sale and distribution of liquor, but personal use was not against the law. Second, alcohol prohibition was not enforced in the way today's drug laws are. Congress and the executive branch were uninterested in enforcing the law. Even many prohibitionists felt that the law was so effective it did not need enforcement. Police, prosecutors, judges and juries frequently refused to use the powers the law gave them. In 1927, only 18 of the 48 states even budgeted money for the enforcement of Prohibition, and some states openly defied the law.

The key difference between alcohol and drug prohibition, however, lies in the substance itself. Alcohol, unlike illegal drugs, has a long history of widespread, accepted use in our society, dating back to before biblical times. Illegal drugs cannot claim such pervasive use by a large part of the planet's population over such a long period of time.

What lessons should we be taking from America's experiment with Prohibition to inform our drug policy? One is that when a substance is legal, powerful business interests have an incentive to encourage use by keeping prices low. Heavier use, in turn, means heavier social costs. For example, alcohol is the cause of 1 million more arrests annually than are all illegal drugs combined. Indeed, alcohol use leads to $180 billion in costs associated with healthcare, the criminal justice system and lost productivity; alcohol taxes, on the other hand—kept

outrageously low by a powerful lobby—generate revenue amounting to less than a tenth of these costs.

Even so, drug legalization advocates try to capitalize on our country's current budget woes and use the potential for new tax revenue as a key argument in favor of repealing drug laws. But as author Daniel Okrent, whose research into Prohibition inspired Burns' series, wrote last year, "The history of the intimate relationship between drinking and taxing suggests . . . that . . . [people] indulging a fantasy of income tax relief emerging from a cloud of legalized marijuana smoke should realize that it is likely only a pipe dream."

If our experience with legal alcohol provides us with any lessons for drug policy, it is this: We have little reason to believe that the benefits of drug legalization would outweigh its costs.

Supporters of marijuana legalization—like this woman attending a rally in Florida in 2010—compare the current war on drugs to Prohibition. Supporters of government policies counter that marijuana and other drugs can't be compared to alcohol. (© Joe Raedle/ Getty Images.)

But that doesn't mean that we need to be severe and punitive in our drug enforcement either. People in recovery from alcohol and other drug addictions should be entitled to social benefits, including access to education, housing and employment opportunities, despite their past drug use. We should think seriously about the rationale and effectiveness of imposing harsh mandatory minimum sentences for simple drug possession. And no one can credibly argue that we have enough treatment slots for everyone who needs them, or that we have an adequate supply of evidence-based drug prevention for every school kid regardless of economic background. Indeed, our current drug policy leaves something to be desired, and like most policies, it needs constant refinement.

Still, it is wrongheaded to think that the only choices we have in drug policy are a punitive approach centered exclusively on enforcement, or one based on careless legalization. Neither has ever worked particularly well.

CHAPTER 3

Personal Narratives

A Man Recalls What It Was Like to Be a Teen During Prohibition

J. Willard Conlon, interviewed by Walter Goodman

In the following viewpoint, J. Willard Conlon, who was in his teens during the Prohibition years, describes how everyone was aware that liquor was being sold in his neighborhood, and no one criticized bootleggers. Some people made it at home using malt that was stocked by grocers in far larger quantities than would be needed to flavor baked goods. Young teens went to speakeasies; Conlon bought his first bottle of bootleg whiskey when he was only sixteen. When a group went together, the waiter would empty bottles of beer into a bucket from which everyone drank. No one he knew was acquainted with any gangsters, but he did hear about local violence. Conlon worked for the federal government, first in the Treasury Department and later as an investigator for the Civil Service Commission and the Justice Department.

SOURCE. J. Willard Conlon, "Memoir (oral history transcript)," University of Illinois, 1972. Copyright © 1972 by the University of Illinois. All rights reserved. Reproduced by permission.

*W*alter Goodman: *During the 1920's you were a teenager. Do you remember much about Prohibition, such as the speakeasies?*

J. Willard Conlon: Sure do. . . . When we came to Springfield [Illinois] . . . there were several corner saloons, as they were called then in our neighborhood because I heard my father refer to them on several occasions. Then later, of course, the prohibition law was passed, and just when that came about escaped my attention as it had no interest for me. I really didn't know a thing about that.

Then still a little later, I became conscious of the fact that the sale of liquor was illegal and all of the saloons and taverns were closed and one thing or another, and that liquor was being sold on, oh, sort of a, well, it's hard to put it—an illegal basis, but that's not it. It was being sold on the sly, I think is the only way you'd say it. And us children and young teenagers, we were pretty well aware of who was doing the selling and who was doing the buying. And it became quite the custom for people to make their own wine and their own beer. And in this, they were, well, they were encouraged, really, by the business interest [in] the purchase of a product called malt. . . . It was sold as something one would use in baking, to flavor bread or flavor other baked products. But any recipe will show you that a tablespoon full of that malt would flavor a large batch of bread, whereas it was sold in about a three-pound can, you see. So that was just really a subterfuge. So it soon became quite the custom that everyone would buy these cans of malt and a package of compressed yeast, and there was a little sugar involved in it, I think. And you put this all in together with water and dissolved it in lukewarm water in a large crock, and that would soon foam up, and then that foam would disappear and then it would revive and foam up again, after which time you'd bottle it. It made a pretty palatable beer; it was really very good. The point here is that every grocery store at that time, they would have on hand at least a half a dozen, and in all probability twelve different varieties of this malt. I doubt very much if you could buy a can of it in Springfield today.

Speakeasies

What about the speakeasies?

> [At a young age] you got to know who was in the business and where you might be able to buy something to drink.

The speakeasies? As I say, we, as youngsters, we knew where they were. It wasn't until a little later on that I patronized any of them, but I actually frequently did. I have been in speakeasies on a number of occasions. As time went on, you got to know who was in the business and where you might be able to buy something to drink, and this started at a rather young age. . . . I know that I was only 16 when I bought my first bottle of white mule, which is the same as bootleg whiskey.

Where were some of these at?

They were scattered, really, all over the town. . . . Some of them sold only a little alcohol that was supposed to be distilled from sugar—it's said that that's a very easy and quick way to make alcohol—and they'd sell you the alcohol and cut it with water for you and sometimes they'd flavor it. By flavor it, I mean they'd make an imitation gin or even put a little peach or blackberry flavoring or something like that. But we had a custom here in Springfield in the sale of this home brew that I have never heard of any place else.

When three or four people would approach a bootlegging joint—say on the north side—you'd go in and all of us would sit at a table, all in one party. And someone would say, "Let's have a beer." The waiter, or sometimes a waitress, would take a large tin bucket, and empty into that bucket two quart bottles of beer and then bring it to us. Then everyone would drink from this bucket and

Clients drink in a speakeasy in New York City in 1932. (© Keystone-France/ Gamma-Keystone via Getty Images.)

pass it around until it was empty, and then it would be the next man's turn and he, too, would order. In other words, you just emptied these bottles into this bucket, and you drank out of it until it was empty and then you ordered another one. If you wanted something a little harder like white mule, as I say, you would get a shot and they'd give you a chaser of soda pop or whatever you wanted.

How much actual public support was there, at least in your family?

I never heard of any real criticism of this, except of a sort of a social nature. By this I mean that there would be some comment, "Well, so-and-so is sending his son off to be a doctor, and he can well afford to because he's been bootlegging for years." That's an actual quotation. I even know the doctor.

How good was the liquor?

It was not very good. There were a lot of scare stories in magazines and in the newspapers—there still is, of course—about people drinking inferior alcohol—wood alcohol was the term we all used—where people went blind and one thing or another. And there was also talk that in the manufacture of this white mule that there'd be dead rats and cats and other matter of that kind in the fermentation vats. And that might well be, but I remember that after Prohibition it came out that a large proportion of this homemade product had been tested and found to be as palatable and as potable as one could expect. In other words, there was not really any great risk to be run from this. It was not as bad as it was painted. . . .

Gang Violence

Did you ever run across anybody you knew who was involved in the gangster element or the violence which occurred in Springfield?

Nobody, as far as being personally acquainted with anyone, not really. I knew a couple of fellows about my own age who it was said were working for the bootleggers and were working for Chicago and Cicero interests, and it might well be. . . .

Could you relate any incidents of violence that occurred in Springfield?

Oh, I well remember when various bootlegging joints were closed down and the gossip was that they had been ordered to close by the syndicate. I don't think we used the word syndicate in those days; I think somebody said, "the gangsters." But at any rate, there was a place out north of town called the Wayside Inn which was pretty notorious for its day because it continued to operate on a little more sophisticated level than the working man's common beer-drinking joint that I talked about. They had a band there, and they had a regular bar, and they had some pretty racy decorations in back of the bar. And it seemed to enjoy a great popularity with the more affluent people in the town, especially those who, oh, liked to swing a little bit, I suppose. At any rate, the word went out they were told to close down, and they didn't do it. They were then burned out; they were definitely bombed, and the place was burned. There were no casualties in that, but the place never did open again.

I remember the first gangster killing that I ever heard of was down on Ninth and Reynolds Street. There was a grocery store and another store there, and apparently two fellows were walking east on Reynolds Street, and as they cornered Ninth Street there were some fellows there waiting for them and they had machine guns, and they killed them right on the spot. Then some time later, there was another killing at a place called the Bluebird Cafe down on Jefferson Street. It was between Seventh and Eighth Street on Jefferson. And it was on the south side of the street, and it was the sort of a place of questionable repute. At any rate, some fellows were sitting in there one afternoon at a table and the place was invaded by other people with machine guns who killed two fellows there. That, by the way, is only a block away from the police station. . . .

How did the police react to the violence or the speakeasies or to any of this stuff that was actually illegal? Were there actually any great moves to eliminate crime?

As far as I know, their attitude was this: they did not condone any of this. This was illegal, and therefore they were against it. But their basic attitude was that this was a Federal law and it's up to the Federal Government to do their own enforcing. . . . My impression—and I was quite young at the time, although, by now, I was in my twenties—was that they felt that the enforcement of the prohibition law, itself, was really not their first responsibility. In an advisory or other capacity, they would help where necessary, but in ferreting out or trying to collect evidence, I don't believe they spent much time on it at all. Now then, there were many, many individual policemen who took the attitude that, well, they didn't approve of prohibition anyway, and they themselves liked to drink a little, and it was not really uncommon to run across an off-duty policeman either in a place of that kind or attending a social function where a good deal of liquor was served.

> There were many, many individual policemen who took the attitude that, well, they didn't approve of prohibition anyway, and they themselves liked to drink a little.

A Law Enforcement Organization Remembers an African American Prohibition Agent

Bureau of Alcohol, Tobacco, Firearms and Explosives

The following viewpoint profiles Eugene Jackson, the first African American prohibition agent who was killed in the line of duty. Despite concern and warning from Jackson's wife, the agent attempted to make a liquor buy and arrest the seller. After finding out Jackson was an agent, the seller took out his gun and fired two shots, killing Jackson. The Bureau of Alcohol, Tobacco, Firearms and Explosives is a law enforcement organization within the United States.

SOURCE. Bureau of Alcohol, Tobacco, Firearms and Explosives, "Remembering Prohibition Agent Killed in the Line of Duty," February 1, 2007. www.atf.gov.

Undoubtedly, life was good for Prohibition Agent Eugene Jackson and his new bride of one month, Lillie. It was July 31, 1932, and the Washington Senators were playing the Chicago White Sox at Comiskey Park. The Senators were ahead by three runs. The Jacksons and their good friend, Narcotics Inspector James Fletcher, dressed in their Sunday finest, were passing the day together waiting to pick up Fletcher's wife at the railroad station.

Jackson had been working as a federal prohibition agent in a temporary status since September 1925. In March 1932, after passing the written exam, he was granted permanent status and with it came a transfer from Washington to Chicago, his first choice for duty office. Not only did he have a job making $2,300 annually in a time when work could be hard to come by, he landed in the hot spot of prohibition enforcement.

As if things couldn't get any better, Fletcher had also recently been granted a transfer from the capital to the Windy City, moving before his wife so that he could settle in and prepare for her arrival. He rented a kitchenette apartment in the same building on South Parkway as the Jacksons. Fletcher's wife was scheduled to arrive on a train that same afternoon, and the three friends were happily anticipating her arrival as well as their exciting new future. All in all, life was good.

> The three friends watched him deliver a package wrapped in a paper bag much the way liquor was frequently packaged.

Shortly after lunch, the three went to the railroad station. When they arrived, Fletcher's wife was not there as expected. They returned home, no doubt disappointed by the mix-up.

A Suspicious Package

Jackson parked his automobile on the street directly in front of his residence. No sooner were the tires on the curb when they saw a man, about 30 years old, walk up to the house two doors down and knock. From inside the car, the three friends watched him deliver a package wrapped in a paper bag much the way liquor was frequently packaged for delivery to the neighborhoods.

"Ten to one he's a bootlegger," said Jackson.

"You got that right," said Fletcher.

"Now boys, it's Sunday," said Jackson's wife.

"I'm gonna go talk to him," Jackson said. "See if I can make a buy."

"Please let it go," Jackson's wife pleaded. "Make your case some other time. It's Sunday!"

"It's my duty, day or night, to make a case against bootleggers. I've got to go."

Before Jackson's wife could protest further, Jackson was out of the automobile and at the man's side.

"Can you get some liquor for me?" If the man was surprised, he didn't show it.

"What makes you think I'm a bootlegger?"

"I just saw you deliver a package. Anybody can tell it was liquor."

"You a prohibition agent?"

"I'm just a colored man from out of town."

"There's colored agents too. Whereabouts you from?"

"Washington D.C. There's my car with the D.C. plates," Jackson gestured at the automobile.

"How much does the colored man from D.C. want?"

"A gallon will do."

"Be back here in a half hour. If I find you're a prohibition agent, though, I'll come back shooting."

By the time Jackson got back to the car, Fletcher had removed his duty revolver from a bag and placed it on the seat next to him. Jackson opened the car door for his wife and offered her his arm. He escorted her out of the car and up the two flights of stairs to their apartment, leaving Fletcher behind in the car.

No sooner had Jackson opened the apartment door than his wife tried to dissuade him from making the arrest.

"I heard what he said, Eugene. I don't like all of that gun talk. I'm frightened."

Eugene did his best to reassure her before he picked up the phone and called his regular partner, Prohibition Investigator Moses Proffitt. When Proffitt didn't answer the phone, he called Prohibition Investigator Smith Wilson, another colleague.

When Jackson asked Wilson for backup, Smith didn't hesitate. "He'll be back in 30 minutes—I'll be there in 20."

The Plan Goes Awry

Outside, unbeknownst to Jackson, the bootlegger, Drew Clark, returned early and pulled alongside of Jackson's car. He held up the jug of liquor for Fletcher to see. "Got it. Where's your friend?"

"Upstairs getting money."

"I can't be hanging around here."

Fletcher, trying his best to help his friend make the case, replied: "He's coming. Just hold your horses."

Clark got out of his car and waited next to Fletcher, who remained seated in the passenger seat. But not another word passed between them.

Satisfied that Wilson was on his way, Eugene hung up the phone and headed for the door.

"At least take your gun," Lillie said.

"Too bulky. He might see it."

"Please, Eugene."

Fletcher's got his gun. "One gun's enough. I don't need any gunplay today," said Jackson, perhaps remembering his involvement in the shooting death of a D.C. gambler in February of that same year and the sticky internal investigation that followed.

And with that he went out the door, leaving his anxious wife behind in the apartment, looking out of the front window onto the street below.

Eugene greeted the landlady on the landing as he passed and briskly strode up to Clark. "You got the liquor?"

"Yup, I do. You got the money?"

"How much for the whole jug?" Jackson reached in his pocket and pulled out the bills to pay him.

As quick as Clark snatched the money and handed Jackson the jug, Jackson pulled out his badge. "Federal prohibition agent," he announced. "You're under arrest."

The Sting Operation Turns Fatal

Clark plucked his revolver out of his pocket and fired two quick shots into Jackson's torso. Jackson fell against Clark's car. The jug shattered, spilling liquor onto the sidewalk. Jackson landed on the running board of the bootlegger's automobile, and lay still.

Fletcher burst out of the car. Clark quickly fired four shots at Fletcher, who fell to the ground behind the automobile and crawled into the road.

Possibly out of bullets, Clark took off running down the street. Fletcher rebounded and quickly jumped into Jackson's automobile to give pursuit.

Fletcher lost sight of Clark around 39th St. and drove back to the scene of the shooting. Only then did he realize how badly injured his friend was. He struggled to load him into the car, and sped off to Provident Hospital at 16 West 36th St.

Meanwhile, Prohibition Agent Smith Wilson arrived according to plan and right on time. But all he saw was Jackson's car with Fletcher behind the wheel speeding down South Parkway. He did what he was trained to do. He cordoned off the crime scene and picked up the pieces of the shattered jug, attempting to mop up the evidence dripping into the gutter.

> A few minutes after arriving at Provident Hospital, Eugene Jackson passed away despite the heroic efforts of the hospital staff.

He recovered two ounces of the liquor and prepared it for shipment to the United States Chemist for analysis.

A few minutes after arriving at Provident Hospital, Eugene Jackson passed away despite the heroic efforts of the hospital staff. His last words were reportedly, "God have mercy on my soul." A little over one week after Prohibition Agent Eugene Jackson was killed in the line of duty, bootlegger Drew Clark was indicted on first degree murder charges.

A Former Prohibition Agent Describes Gathering Evidence of Bootlegging

Lloyd Jester, interviewed by Miriam Feingold

In the following viewpoint, Lloyd Jester describes the process of gathering evidence against bootleggers during Prohibition. To get a federal search warrant he had to have evidence obtained through the natural senses—such as sight, hearing, and smell—that liquor was being manufactured or sold, and such evidence was not always easy to obtain. When it was lacking, they took the case to state court, which had less strict requirements. Jester explains that agents concentrated on manufacturing, because one such raid could eliminate far more illegal liquor than closing down a place where it was sold. Jester was a federal prohibition agent and later became an inspector in the Alameda County District Attorney's Office in California.

SOURCE. Lloyd Jester, "Reminiscences of an Inspector in the District Attorney's Office," *Perspectives on the Alameda County District Attorney's Office*, vol. 2, no. 5. University of California, Bancroft Library, 1972. Copyright © 1972 by the University of California. All rights reserved. Reproduced by permission.

Lloyd Jester: It was in May of '29 that I went into the Department of Justice, Bureau of Prohibition. I was sent from Los Angeles to San Francisco and I was in the San Francisco office for a while. . . . We were making some bootleg raids around Emeryville. I think I'll give you some photographs here, and let you look at them. They are the "joints"—bootleg places in Emeryville. You never saw a "blind pig" bootleg "joint," did you? . . .

A federal prohibition agent could take the particular case arrest into the local court or he could take the accused into the federal court, either one. As a rule it was his choice to make.

Miriam Feingold: How did you decide?

Well usually this was governed by the type of the case. Now, at that time, by state law the query was not, "How did you get your evidence?", but rather it was, "What evidence have you got?". . . In other words, if you'd come in with evidence of a crime having been committed, the state courts didn't go into the proposition of "How did you get this evidence? How did you come about having this in your possession?", but rather they just said, "Well, here's the evidence, and there's the guilty party."

In the federal court, however, we were bound by the Fourth and the Fifth Amendments, all of the constitutional amendments, in fact. You had to get this evidence without violating, in the slightest degree, any one of these possible constitutional rights. Now the only way that you could get [evidence of] a crime committed in your presence according to the federal rules, was by the use of one of your five natural senses, which was feel, taste, smell, sight, and hearing. If the particular thing happened within your hearing or you saw it happen and so forth in your presence by use of any one or all of those natural senses then the crime could be [viewed as] committed in your presence.

Getting Evidence

For example, let's take a still, one that was located out in the country like this picture, see. Here's a gate and it says "No Trespassing" and so forth, see? The still is in a barn, way back in the back there where you can't see it from the road. Here's the close-up of the barn taken after we got in and made our case.

Yes, you wouldn't even know that there was anything going on there.

No. So how would you be able to raid this still, and obviously we did because here's the pictures of it in the barn, as proof. How would you be able to raid this?

Well, here's one procedure. They, the operators, had to have supplies going into this still and they had to haul the produce out. Some of the supplies were these five gallon cans that you see here in this photo, these five gallon cans were used to haul the alcohol, the produce out. They would have to go in empty and come out full, wouldn't they?

Yes.

Sugar would have to go in and yeast would have to go in to make the mash. We could follow a truck from a sugar distributing point or from the Continental Can Company or the American Can Company or wherever, to some farming place like shown here in this photo. If it was cans we knew they wouldn't be feeding the cans to the hogs! If it was sugar, it was a possibility, you know, possible but not probable.

In this case you'd have to use two or three probable causes. Now if you could get an odor of the fermenting mash this would, added to the cans and sugar going in, be probable cause. So you could go all around the area, up in the hills, drive around at late and unusual hours or in the early morning hours, usually when the air was heavy, to try to get an odor of fermenting mash. That would be one natural sense, "smell."

Now that you have already seen the cans going in and obtained an odor of mash, if a load of alcohol cans came out and it went someplace—say to Emeryville or to a garage in San Francisco or anywhere, and you had the good fortune to be able to follow it and see the alcohol in the terminal, or maybe an arrest would be made there by local authorities to prove it was alcohol coming out, then you'd have a good federal case. But you would still have to get a search warrant; you used your natural senses for probable cause for the warrant. To get a search warrant in federal court you have to particularly describe the places to be searched and the things to be seized. This is hard to do, as anyone will agree. . . .

> To get a search warrant in federal court you have to particularly describe the places to be searched and the things to be seized.

Now if this were a state case, if you were going to take this case into state court, in those days, all you had to do was wait your opportunity, go over the fence, go on in and "knock the thing over"—this was a term used for raid in those days. Then make your arrests, make your seizure, the court would only ask, "What evidence do you have?" and not, "How did you get it?" You see that was the difference in those days.

The same thing would apply towards bootleg joints, a bar catering to the public. When you'd see bootleg joints running, with the barred doors, peep holes, etc., people going in sober and coming out under the influence, you didn't need a Ouija board to tell you that it was a bootleg joint, although the law was still quite a sticky wicket on that subject as far as the federal law was concerned. In many of these cases we'd go in and knock it over on the state proposition and we'd take it into state court and be done with it. . . .

You didn't have to have as strict standards of evidence?

No, no. The evidence that you produced in court was what counted, at least in those days, not how you came by it.

Manufacture of Alcohol

This [*shows picture*] is what's called a "cutting plant." Here is where they take the alcohol that comes in the five gallon can and mix it with distilled water in these barrels, see. If it's going to be whiskey, they'll color it with burnt sugar and so forth and with coloration. There is an electrical rod, an aging bar. An electric cord comes on it. . . .

That gets very hot. They put that down through the bung in the barrel. They put it in tight. This heat from this

Prohibition agents pour liquor into a sewer following a raid on a New York City bootlegging operation in 1921. (© **Buyenlarge/ Getty Images.**)

rod is supposed to age it, age this whiskey. Now if they want gin, why they just put juniper berries in, cut [it] with water, and to hell with it! They don't age that. But they could make scotch and all other types, you know, in these barrels. That's called a "cutting plant." From there the bootleggers bottle it. There were four steps in the production and sale of bootleg liquor. It went from the still, to the cutting plant, to the bootlegger and joint, to the customer.

Then you see the stills. This still was like this first [*shows picture of undamaged still*] and when we got through with it we chopped it up. . . .

There were some dangerous cases where they used an old hot water heater for a coil. Here's what it looks like when we got through chopping it up.

This is for the cooking. They have the pot itself up on bricks here, the copper pot, and they have a stove heater under there that puts the fire and heat to it. The flame heats it up and causes the mash to evaporate and the evaporation goes up through the copper baffle plates in the column. There are little divisions it has to go through. Each division has a certain number of holes with little copper cups over the top of each. This catches the evaporation (steam). Finally it cools enough and drops as liquid, goes into the "try" box. From that it is put into the cans. A "try" box is where they gauge the percentage of alcohol. . . .

> The federal government and the Prohibition agents, by and large, were out after the source of supply, that is, the stills and the cutting plants.

Some of [the stills] are tremendous in size and would turn out a heck of a lot of alcohol a day.

The still was the source of supply, and the federal government and the Prohibition agents, by and large, were out after the source of supply, that is, the stills and the cutting plants and that sort of thing.

However, the general public, at least the WCTU [Woman's Christian Temperance Union], the churches, etc., was making such a ruckus and hollering about the bootleg joints so that you had to go in there and make a big splurge, knock off a few bootleg joints and satisfy the general public and the church folks, see. But I can point out to you this, that if we knocked over one great big still . . . that was turning out several thousand gallons of 190 proof alky [alcohol] a day at the source of supply, we were doing a better job even though it took us a longer while to locate and to make a powerful enough case to satisfy the federal court. We did more good that way than going out and knocking over dozens of these bootleg joints a night! . . .

Arresting Bootleggers

Why did we do it? Well, here's Earl Warren [who later became chief justice of the Supreme Court], here in Alameda County, a very vigorous prosecutor, a politician responding to the church and WCTU folks. Therefore, he's got his own active staff set up to go out and raid these places. The federal courts were charged with the responsibility, regardless of how large or small it was that is, to enforce Prohibition.

In the spirit of cooperation with Mr. Warren and with his people, we would get together and we'd go out and we'd raid these places, or if I and my crew went out alone and raided the place we would turn the case over to the state. Because the federal government wasn't in the business of making money from the fines, turning a case over to the local court was never questioned. It is still a fact that in the small towns . . . they depended a heck of a lot upon these fines they received from these Prohibition cases to help them in their expenses of government. They never admitted it then and many deny it now, but it's the truth. . . .

The Judge [would] come down in the middle of the nighttime, and he waxed eloquent. He dispensed judgments in all directions. Everybody who'd come in was guilty and then he had a set fine of $250 or whatever it was. This is in Depression days and that's a pretty good size of money. It didn't take many of these bootleggers to build the coffers of the city up to the point where it paid the Judge's salary for a year. . . .

> [Bootleggers] could stand so many knockovers a year, pay their fines the same as buying a license.

[Bootleggers] could stand so many knockovers a year, pay their fines the same as buying a license, and think no more of it.

But if you arrested them more than three times, they'd start screaming like a banshee. They would say things like, "Gee, you're getting me all the time! Why aren't you getting so-and-so?" But they didn't mind coming in and paying up a fine once in a while. What they feared most was more than three convictions on one place, which meant facing a chance of abatement [removal of property as a public nuisance].

I remember one time we had a fellow by the nickname of "Peanuts." I don't know what his real name was. He was a bartender. . . . Well it was no fun arresting "Peanuts" towards the end, because you could just as well knock at the front door and say, "Peanuts, come on out. I'm going to take you in and book you." And he'd do it! So there was no sport in it anymore, and I suppose that that's why "Peanuts" went so long between arrests.

Making Bootleg Wine in California

Vivienne Sosnowski

In the following viewpoint, Vivienne Sosnowski tells the story of Italian American winegrowers who lost their means of earning a living during Prohibition. Sosnowski describes what Lou Colombano told her about his family's experience. For a period of time his father and uncle made bootleg wine and brandy on their farms, and his father allowed another bootlegger to operate a large still on his land. But they gave the venture up when it became too risky for their families. Sosnowski has been an editorial director of newspapers, including the *Washington Examiner* and the *San Francisco Examiner*. She is the author of *When the Rivers Ran Red*; which this viewpoint is excerpted from.

The Colombano family's experience with bootlegging was one that was played out many times. At first it was a small enterprise; later it grew in size until the family feared for their lives and their freedom, explained Lou Colombano who was born in 1915, five years before Prohibition became law.

"My parents, Eligio and Angela, were married in 1913," said Colombano. "They had come here together from Piedmont in Italy. Eligio had been in the United States on an earlier trip and then he'd returned to Italy to marry. His brother Camillo had arrived in San Francisco after the big earthquake"—the 1906 quake and fire that leveled much of that great city. . . . Camillo ran a wine and brandy emporium in North Beach. A photo of Camillo taken at that time shows a strikingly handsome young man perched on an immaculately kept wagon, freshly painted with lavish decorative script. The photo shows the wagon full of five-gallon wine demijohns and drawn by two dark horses—one of them named Blackie—standing poised to deliver wine. The demijohns are wrapped in raffia in the style in which Chianti bottles once were.

But a business founded in such promise in the years after the earthquake did not have long to prosper before Prohibition stopped it in its tracks. "When the country went dry," Colombano explained in 2008, "my uncle said, 'I'm out of business. I can't make a living.'

"My father had been a farmer in Italy. He understood grapes. And he knew how to make wine. So my uncle suggested to my father that they should go north and find some land—hopefully somewhere near Asti, which was where the biggest winery was then," said Colombano. The brothers believed the owners of the Italian Swiss Colony operation would have bought fine land and that they would do well to be close to it.

A Good Living

The two Colombano brothers did find a suitable ranch near Asti, about 80 miles north of San Francisco, and promptly planted a vineyard of about 30 acres. Before long, Eligio was making good red wine and Camillo was trucking it down to San Francisco in the middle of the night. And the two black delivery horses that used to trot through the hilly city streets of San Francisco had been trucked to the ranch and were now pulling plows.

"Camillo drove a green Chandler touring car," remembered Colombano. "The car was full of tanks made to carry wine and brandy—but the tanks had been constructed, then upholstered to look exactly like the bottoms and backs of seats.

> 'The car was full of tanks made to carry wine and brandy . . . upholstered to look exactly like the bottoms and backs of seats.'

"Dad and my uncle made a pretty good living. Yes, they were doing pretty well. My father said his share of the business was $55 a month."

Like most farm families, Colombano said, "we also had cows, pigs, chickens, vegetable gardens. We made our own cheese and butter and once a week, made bread in the outdoor oven. But we didn't yet have electricity on the farm."

The business was such a success that the car's secret holding tanks were soon inadequate for the demand, so the brothers "bought a truck to carry their wine and grappa [grape-based brandy] and they'd set off from the winery with the barrels covered with oat sacks," Colombano said.

Their first run-in with trouble both surprised and infuriated them. Said Colombano, "Two guys came in the middle of the night to the ranch and told us they were Prohibition officers and that our truck was confiscated." One of the supposed government agents drove off with the truck full of wine and grappa; the other hung around the Colombano home all day before he finally left. The men were never seen again—and had nothing to do with the government. "Eventually the truck was found abandoned in San Rafael, a few miles from the Sausalito-San Francisco ferry with nothing on it," Colombano said.

Men operate a grape press for making wine in the Italian colony of San Francisco, California, during Prohibition. (© American Stock Archive/Archive Photos/Getty Images.)

The armed men had been hijackers, not Prohibition agents.

Given the night work and the worry of an official raid at any time, Colombano's parents eventually grew tired of bootlegging and closed their business. Camillo bought a ranch at Morgan Hill, about 200 miles south of Geyserville, where he established a vineyard of Carignane. Eligio resettled a few miles away in Geyserville, establishing a new farm and raising grapes and prunes. Everyone contributed to the family's well being.

"I even had a little milk route. We had extra milk from our cows. When I got back from school every evening I used to get on my bike and deliver to six or seven customers. I used to sell it for 10 cents a quart."

But the lure of the wine business, so much a part of the Colombano family's heritage, was too powerful to ignore. Eligio Colombano decided again to make and sell wine illegally, and soon he decided to add to his inventory. He was going to make grappa as well. Eligio bought a still and took advantage of his new property's fortunate geography to defy the government. "In winter, the river used to come up around the farm," Lou recalled of his teenage years. "We couldn't get to school and nobody could get to our ranch." It was a perfect situation for a bootlegger.

> The lure of the wine business, so much a part of the Colombano family's heritage, was too powerful to ignore.

"My dad would work the still all day and I would work it at night." His father's wine and grappa "sold locally or to folk who would come up in the good months of year from San Francisco to buy a gallon of grappa for $1.50, or to get a gallon or two of wine. If you bought your own jug, wine was 25 cents a gallon."

Business flourished yet again. . . .

A New Venture

Even though Eligio's still was contributing healthy sums to the family coffers, one day he got a bigger and better offer that made the idea of running his own small still pale in comparison.

Eligio's brother Camillo had a friend named Palosi, "a big-time bootlegger, big-time. And he came to see my dad at the ranch." Palosi had heard the Colombanos lived on a dead-end road with no through traffic. "So he came to my dad with a deal. He said, 'If you let me put a still in your big barn, I'll give you $50 a day for every day we run it.'

"My mother was terrified. She thought we'd be found out by Prohibition agents and lose everything we had. But we'd had a terrible frost that spring, which took all our grapes. Everything got burnt by the frost—there was just no crop that year. My father had said he would not be able to pay his property tax. So when Palosi made the offer, well, my father felt he had to accept for the good of his family."

Palosi required a large barn well out of the way of prying eyes. He had recently acquired—he did not explain how—a huge supply of port, which was sitting padlocked in a winery about a mile from the Colombano farm; he needed not only a still to convert the port into grappa but a place to store it; then, when the times were right, he would get it moved down to San Francisco.

"Well, we knew where the winery was that he was talking about," said Colombano. It was the winery of a family they knew in Geyserville, located near the Hoffman House. . . .

Money was no object to Palosi, it appeared. The project required running a two-inch galvanized tin pipeline underground from the winery to the large new still under construction in the Colombano barn, a distance of over a mile.

"He had men dig all night and they even dug right under the railway track, which had a fair amount of traffic on it. My mother would feed the hordes of workers it took to do this, and they slept at our house on cots."

Then came a serious, possibly deal-ending glitch in the plan.

"Palosi found out that we didn't have electricity to the farm yet. And he needed it desperately for the turbines that were going to cook the port." The solution took time to engineer, because the Colombano farm's geography—so convenient for hiding a still—also placed it some distance from the nearest power lines. Once again Palosi revealed considerable business acumen. He spliced into the nearest power line of the electric company that serviced Geyserville, running power all the way to the still via a line burrowed into the ground next to the already constructed galvanized wine pipeline.

That electric company and its shareholders was unknowingly but effectively subsidizing one of the largest stills in the county.

Palosi's still was huge: At a time when many stills were about the size of a baby's bath and held five gallons of liquid, this one stretched 10 or 12 feet in diameter—about the volume of a medium-size room.

Now that the pipeline was dug and camouflaged and the power was in, it was time to start up the still. The Colombanos were by turns stunned then terrified at the noise.

"It made a terrible roar," remembers Colombano. "Terrible."

"You could hear it everywhere, we thought. We had one neighbor to the side of us, who must have heard it but never said a thing."

"My mother was hardly sleeping by then, she was so scared."

Risky Business

But the gambit had worked. Grappa poured out of the still in an endless stream day and night. Palosi's crew could fill a five-gallon can, kept camouflaged by hay in the barn, in just a few minutes.

"There were three shifts each day and four people were needed on each shift. Twelve people in all, each day, were working on it, and my mother struggled so hard feeding them, but they did purchase all the food for her to cook." The liquor was taken away to San Francisco at night. . . .

Colombano's dad was making his $50 a day for the use of the barn, and the still had been operating 24 hours a day for 10 days, when Palosi suddenly announced that operations would cease immediately.

"I'm going to send a crew in," he said. "We have to get this thing out of here in 24 hours."

Palosi had received a tip from one of his paid informants that the barn was to be raided. They had only a day to erase all traces of the giant still. It seemed impossible. First, the vast copper pot, with its chimney and all the cooking and evaporating paraphernalia, had to be completely taken apart, piece by piece; and then there were the cans, some empty, many filled and hidden under straw. The staff, their cots—everything had to vanish by the next day.

"But, by God, they did it," said Colombano. "They worked and worked and in 24 hours every single thing was gone from the barn. The only things left from the operation were the pipeline and the electrical connections. But the Prohibition agents missed those completely when they visited."

Eligio and Angela decided that their family ranch would not be involved in bootlegging again.

Like other bootleggers, they had heard tell of the mighty force the Bureau of Internal Revenue's Prohibition Unit (it would be renamed the Bureau of Prohibition in 1927) had arrayed against them. Breaking Prohibition law was hazardous.

GLOSSARY

AAPA
The Association Against the Prohibition Amendment, a leading organization working toward the repeal of Prohibition.

Anti-Saloon League
The leading organization that lobbied in favor of Prohibition.

bathtub gin
Low-quality liquor made by amateurs, often at home. It was not made in bathtubs; the name arose from the use of tub faucets to top off the bottles when sink faucets were not tall enough.

blind pig or blind tiger
A low-class establishment that illegally sold liquor, usually without also offering food.

bone-dry
State or local laws stricter than the national prohibition law —for example, those that banned consumption as well as sale, or that did not allow purchase of wine for sacramental purposes.

bootlegger
A person who illegally transported and/or sold liquor.

denatured alcohol
Alcohol to which an obnoxious—or even poisonous—substance had been added for the sole purpose of discouraging people from drinking it. During Prohibition the government required all industrial alcohol to be denatured.

dry
As an adjective, a territory in which the sale of liquor was illegal; as a noun, a person who favored Prohibition.

hip flask
A flat container for liquor, shaped to be worn on the person. Though these existed long before Prohibition, their use became common during that era.

John Barleycorn
A personification of liquor made from grain. On the night before Prohibition went into effect, many cities held public "funerals" for John Barleycorn.

moonshiner A person who illegally manufactured liquor for sale. The term was applied to those in cities as well as those in isolated country areas.

Noble Experiment A term by which Prohibition is sometimes referred because President Herbert Hoover was misquoted as having called it that in opposing its repeal. Hoover actually said it was a "social and economic experiment, noble in motive and far-reaching in purpose." He strongly objected to the misquote.

Rum Row An area on the Atlantic Coast where rum-running was especially common.

rumrunner A person who illegally smuggled liquor into the country, or a ship used for that purpose.

saloon An establishment where liquor was served to working-class men in the era before Prohibition, many of whom spent their wages on liquor and then mistreated their families. Saloons were often centers of vice and political corruption.

speakeasy An upscale establishment that illegally served alcoholic drinks, usually also offering food and/or entertainment. A password was often required for entry.

temperance Originally referred to moderation in the use of alcohol, but came to mean total abstinence.

Volstead Act The federal law establishing penalties for violation of the Eighteenth Amendment.

WCTU Woman's Christian Temperance Union, an organization founded in the nineteenth century that advocated Prohibition along with other social reforms.

wet As an adjective, a territory in which the sale of liquor was legal or where it was readily obtainable despite illegality; as a noun, a person who opposed Prohibition.

Wickersham Commission A federal commission established in 1931 to study the possibility of repealing the Eighteenth Amendment. Despite acknowledging that Prohibition could not be enforced, it recommended against repeal, favoring instead a revision of the amendment.

WONPR Women's Organization for National Prohibition Reform, an organization founded in 1929 that was instrumental in bringing about the repeal of Prohibition.

wood alcohol Methanol, a poisonous substance used to denature alcohol. Few, if any, people drank pure denatured alcohol, but some bootleggers mixed it with liquor; any contaminated liquor was commonly called wood alcohol.

CHRONOLOGY

1851   Maine becomes the first state to pass a prohibition law.

1887   The Supreme Court rules in *Mugler v. Kansas* that states have the power to pass and enforce prohibition laws. Two have already done so, and by the time the Eighteenth Amendment goes into effect, thirty-three states, covering 63 percent of the total population, are "dry."

1890   Congress enacts the Wilson Original Packages Act. It states that all intoxicating beverages shipped interstate will be subject to the laws of the destination state upon arrival but does not authorize federal enforcement.

1893   May 24: The Anti-Saloon League is founded by Howard H. Russell. This organization becomes a major force in raising support for national prohibition.

1913   March 1: Congress passes the Webb-Kenyon bill over the veto of President William H. Taft, who believes it to be unconstitutional due to conflict with the Commerce Clause. This law prohibits interstate transportation of liquor if it is intended to be sold, used, or possessed in a state where that is unlawful.

        December 10: The Committee of One Thousand presents a proposed amendment for national prohibition to Congress.

1914   December 22: The House of Representatives votes 197 to 190 for national prohibition, but the bill fails to pass because the necessary two-thirds majority is lacking.

1917   January 8: The Supreme Court rules that the Webb-
        Kenyon bill is constitutional.

        March 3: The Reed "Bone-Dry" Amendment to a post
        office appropriation bill becomes law. It prohibits per-
        sonal importation of liquor into states that prohibit its
        manufacture and sale even when those states' laws allow
        individuals to bring it in for personal use. It also bans
        alcohol advertising in such states. However, there is no
        provision for federal enforcement.

        April 4: The bill that becomes the Eighteenth
        Amendment is introduced into Congress.

        May 18: Congress prohibits the sale of intoxicating
        liquor to soldiers and on October 6 extends this prohi-
        bition to the navy.

        August 1: The Eighteenth Amendment bill is passed by
        the Senate.

        August 10: As a war measure, Congress prohibits the
        use of foodstuff or feeds in the production of distilled
        spirits for beverages.

        December 8: As a war measure designed to reserve
        food, President Woodrow Wilson prohibits the produc-
        tion of most beer.

        December 18: After passing in the House on the previ-
        ous day, the final version of the Eighteenth Amendment
        is adopted by the Senate and submitted to the states for
        ratification.

1918   January 8: The Eighteenth Amendment is ratified by
        Missouri, the first state to do so.

September 6: The Agricultural Appropriation Bill is passed, prohibiting the manufacture of beer and wine after May 1, 1919, and forbidding the sale of any liquor after June 30, 1919.

November 12: The Association Against the Prohibition Amendment (AAPA) is founded by William H. Stayton. Later, this organization is to be instrumental in bringing about repeal.

November 21: Ten days after the World War I armistice, President Wilson signs the Wartime Prohibition Act (passed by Congress on August 29), which prohibits the use of foodstuff to produce any form of alcoholic beverage until the end of demobilization.

1919   January 16: The Eighteenth Amendment is ratified by Nebraska, the last state needed for it to become law. It is formally certified as ratified on January 29.

July 1: The Wartime Prohibition Act goes into effect.

October 28: Congress passes the National Prohibition Act, also known as the Volstead Act, over President Wilson's veto.

1920   January 6: The Supreme Court rules that although beer containing a mere half of 1 percent alcohol is not intoxicating and the Eighteenth Amendment concerns only intoxicating beverages, banning it under the Volstead Act is legal because it is incidental to the general power to ban beer.

January 16: The Eighteenth Amendment and the Volstead Act go into effect.

June 7: In a group of cases known as the National

Prohibition Cases, the Supreme Court rules that the Eighteenth Amendment does not violate any provisions of the US Constitution.

July 24: The Internal Revenue Bureau issues a ruling lifting the ban on home brewing of cider and wine containing more than a half of 1 percent alcohol, provided it is "non-intoxicating in fact" and is consumed only in the home.

1923   April 30: The Supreme Court rules that the Eighteenth Amendment applies to both domestic and foreign ships while in US waters, and liquor carried into US waters by foreign ships can be seized even if sealed for use elsewhere. This means passenger ships have to dump any liquor not consumed during the voyage overboard before reaching port. The court also holds, however, that US ships are not subject to Prohibition when on the high seas or in foreign ports, which allows them to compete successfully with foreign ships and leads to the birth of the cruise industry.

1925   March 2: The Supreme Court rules in *Carroll v. United States* that automobiles can be searched without a warrant if there is probable cause to believe they are transporting liquor.

1926   April: Congressional hearings on the National Prohibition Law are held, at which it is argued that beer and wine would be legal under the Eighteenth Amendment and that the law should be modified to allow them.

May 8: President Calvin Coolidge issues an executive order making state, county, and municipal officers federal officials for enforcing Prohibition.

November 29: The Supreme Court rules that Congress

has the power to regulate prescription of wine and spirituous liquor for medicinal purposes. This is a controversial decision viewed by the public as a violation of physicians' rights.

1927   March 3: Congress passes the Bureau of Prohibition Act, effective April 1, which moves enforcement from the Department of Internal Revenue to the Department of the Treasury. It places prohibition field agents under Civil Service and 59 percent of them fail the Civil Service examination.

December 12: A group of prominent men meet and decide to revive the Association Against the Prohibition Amendment and launch a campaign for repeal, although it seems unlikely to succeed.

1928   June 4: In *Olmstead v. United States*, the Supreme Court upholds the use of warrantless wiretapping as a means of obtaining evidence against bootleggers, even when wiretapping is illegal in the state in which it is done. Thus, prohibition agents are authorized to break the law.

November: In the presidential election, Alfred E. Smith, who favors repeal, opposes Herbert Hoover, a strong supporter of Prohibition. Despite the waning public support for Prohibition, Hoover wins.

1929   March 22: The Canadian rumrunner *I'm Alone* is sunk by the US Coast Guard in waters beyond US jurisdiction, setting off an international incident.

May 8: The Women's Organization for National Prohibition Reform (WONPR) is founded by Pauline Sabin, who later appears on the cover of *Time* magazine.

1931   January 7: The Wickersham Commission Report on Alcohol Prohibition is published. It points out that enforcement is failing, but nevertheless opposes repeal.

1932   July 2: In his speech accepting the Democratic Party nomination for president of the United States, Franklin D. Roosevelt endorses repeal of the Eighteenth Amendment, congratulating the convention for having made repeal part of the party's platform. This has a significant effect on public opinion.

1933   February 14: The bill proposing the Twenty-first Amendment is introduced into Congress. It is passed by the Senate two days later and by the House four days after that, on February 20.

March 23: President Roosevelt signs into law an amendment to the Volstead Act known as the Cullen-Harrison Act, which allows the manufacture and sale of light beer and light wine. Sale of beer resumes on April 7.

April 10: Michigan ratifies the Twenty-first Amendment, the first state to do so.

December 5: The Twenty-first Amendment is ratified by Utah, the last state needed, and national prohibition ends. (However, as the amendment gives states the right to make their own liquor laws, in some states the prohibition of alcohol continues.) Roosevelt issues a presidential proclamation announcing repeal and urging the public to buy liquor only from licensed dealers, to observe state prohibition laws, to oppose the return of the saloon, and to avoid using alcohol excessively.

FOR FURTHER READING

Books

The Anti-Prohibition Manual. Cincinnati, OH: National Association of Distillers and Wholesale Dealers, 1918.

Herbert Asbury, *The Great Illusion: An Informal History of Prohibition.* Garden City, NY: Doubleday, 1950.

Edward Behr, *Prohibition: Thirteen Years That Changed America.* New York: Arcade, 1996.

Lamar T. Beman, ed., *Selected Articles on Prohibition of the Liquor Traffic.* White Plains, NY: Wilson, 1917.

Jack S. Blocker, *American Temperance Movements: Cycles of Reform.* Boston: Twayne, 1989.

Karen Blumenthal, *Bootleg: Murder, Moonshine, and the Lawless Years of Prohibition.* New York: Roaring Brook Press, 2011.

Eric Burns, *The Spirits of America: A Social History of Alcohol.* Philadelphia, PA: Temple University Press, 2004.

Edward Butts, *Outlaws of the Lakes: Bootlegging and Smuggling from Colonial Times to Prohibition.* Holt, MI: Thunder Bay Press, 2004.

Sean Cashman, *Prohibition: The Lie of the Land.* New York: Free Press, 1981.

Norman H. Clark, *Deliver Us from Evil: An Interpretation of American Prohibition.* New York: Norton, 1976.

Larry Engleman, *Intemperance: The Lost War Against Liquor.* New York: Free Press, 1979.

Allan S. Everest, *Rum Across the Border: The Prohibition Era in Northern New York.* Syracuse, NY: Syracuse University Press, 1978.

Fabian Franklin, *What Prohibition Has Done to America*. New York: Harcourt Brace, 1922.

J.C. Furnas, *The Life and Times of the Late Demon Rum*. New York: Putnam, 1965.

Richard F. Hamm, *Shaping the Eighteenth Amendment: Temperance Reform, Legal Culture, and the Polity, 1880–1920*. Chapel Hill: University of North Carolina Press, 1995.

Paul R. Kavieff, *The Violent Years: Prohibition and the Detroit Mobs*. Fort Lee, NJ: Barricade Books, 2007.

K. Austin Kerr, *Organized for Prohibition: A New History of the Anti-Saloon League*. New Haven, CT: Yale University Press, 1985.

John Kobler, *Ardent Spirits: The Rise and Fall of Prohibition*. New York: Putnam, 1973.

David E. Kyvig, *Repealing National Prohibition*. Chicago: University of Chicago Press, 1979.

Michael A. Lerner, *Dry Manhattan: Prohibition in New York City*. Cambridge, MA: Harvard University Press, 2007.

Philip P. Mason, *Rumrunning and the Roaring Twenties: Prohibition on the Michigan-Ontario Waterway*. Detroit, MI: Wayne State University Press, 1995.

Mark H. Moore and Dean R. Gerstein, eds., *Alcohol and Public Policy: Beyond the Shadow of Prohibition*. Washington, DC: National Academy Press, 1981.

Kenneth M. Murchison, *Federal Criminal Law Doctrines: The Forgotten Influence of National Prohibition*. Durham, NC: Duke University Press, 1994.

Catherine Gilbert Murdock, *Domesticating Drink: Women, Men, and Alcohol in America, 1870–1940*. Baltimore, MD: Johns Hopkins University Press, 1998.

Arthur Newsholme, *Prohibition in America and its Relation to the Problem of Public Control of Personal Conduct*. London: P.S. King, 1922.

Daniel Okrent, *Last Call: The Rise and Fall of Prohibition*. New York: Scribner, 2010.

Garrett Peck, *The Prohibition Hangover: Alcohol in America from Demon Rum to Cult Cabernet*. New Brunswick, NJ: Rutgers University Press, 2009.

Garrett Peck, *Prohibition in Washington, D.C.: How Dry We Weren't*. Charleston, SC: History Press, 2011.

Thomas R. Pegram, *Battling Demon Rum: The Struggle for a Dry America, 1800–1933*. Chicago: Ivan R. Dee, 1998.

Prohibiting Intoxicating Beverages: Hearings before the Senate Subcommittee of the Committee on the Judiciary. Washington, DC: GPO, 1919.

Kenneth D. Rose, *American Women and the Repeal of Prohibition*. New York: New York University Press, 1996.

Vivienne Sosnowski, *When the Rivers Ran Red: An Amazing Story of Courage and Triumph in America's Wine Country*. New York: Macmillan, 2009.

Charles Stelzle, *Why Prohibition!* New York: Doran, 1918.

Charles Hanson Towne, *The Rise and Fall of Prohibition: The Human Side of What the Eighteenth Amendment and the Volstead Act Have Done to the United States*. New York: Macmillan, 1923.

S. Warner, ed., *Winning Orations in the National Contests of the Intercollegiate Prohibition Association*. Chicago: Intercollegiate Prohibition Association, 1915.

Malcolm F. Willoughby, *Rum War at Sea*. Washington, DC: US Coast Guard, 1964.

Clarence True Wilson and Deets Pickett, *The Case for Prohibition: Its Past, Present Accomplishments, and Future in America*. New York: Funk & Wagnalls, 1923.

Periodicals and Internet Souces

Jacob M. Appel, "'Physicians Are Not Bootleggers': The Short, Peculiar Life of the Medicinal Alcohol Movement," *Bulletin of the History of Medicine*, 2008.

Deborah Blum, "The Chemists' War: The Little-Told Story of How the U.S. Government Poisoned Alcohol During Prohibition with Deadly Consequences," *Slate*, February 19, 2010. www.slate.com.

Donald J. Boudreaux, "Alcohol, Prohibition and the Revenuers," *Freeman*, January 2008. www.thefreemanonline.org.

"The Dry Years: Selected Images Relating to Prohibition from the Collections of the Library of Congress." www.loc.gov.

Richard M. Evans, "How Alcohol Prohibition Was Ended." www.druglibrary.org.

Whidden Graham, "After National Prohibition, What?," *North American Review*, April 1917.

David Greenburg, "Tanked: How New York Dealt with the 'Noble Experiment,'" *Bookforum*, June/July 2007.

Richard Hamm, "American Prohibitionists and Violence, 1865–1920." www.druglibrary.org.

David J. Hanson, "Prohibition: The Noble Experiment." www2.potsdam.edu/handsondj/FunFacts/Prohibition.html.

Jackson Kuhl, "Eight Million Sots in the Naked City: How Prohibition was Imposed on, and Rejected by, New York," *Reason*, November 2007. www.reason.com.

David E. Kyvig, "Women Against Prohibition," *American Quarterly*, 1976.

Theodore B. Lacey, "The Supreme Court's Fluctuating Reaction to National Prohibition in Fourth Amendment Decisions from 1920–1933." http://web.princeton.edu.

Margot Opdycke Lamme, "Tapping into War: Leveraging World War I in the Drive for a Dry Nation," *American Journalism*, no. 4, 2004.

Literary Digest, "End of Prohibition in the United States," November 18, 1933. www.1920-30.com.

John Cole McKim, "Prohibition versus Christianity," *North American Review*, July 1918.

Caryn E. Neumann, "The End of Gender Solidarity: The History of the Women's Organization for National Prohibition Reform in the United States, 1929–1933," *Journal of Women's History*, 1997.

Daniel Okrent, "'Medicinal' Alcohol Made Mockery of Prohibition," *Los Angeles Times*, May 19, 2010.

Emily C. Owens, "The (Not So) Roaring '20s," *New York Times*, October 1, 2011.

J. Petrillo, "Rum Running in the North Country During Prohibition," Adirondack Roots Project, 2001. http://faculty.platts burgh.edu/jay.petrillo/background%20info%20page.htm.

K. Jacob Ruppert, "In Re John Barleycorn: The Role of NYCLA in the Repeal of Prohibition," *New York County Lawyer*, October 2005.

Senate Judiciary Committee Hearings on National Prohibition, April 5–24, 1926. www.druglibrary.org.

Nancy Galey Skogland, "The *I'm Alone* Case: A Tale from the Days of Prohibition," *University of Rochester Library Bulletin*, Spring 1968. www.lib.rochester.edu.

Jacob Sullum, "Prohibition Was Not an Awful Flop," *Reason*, September 7, 2005. www.reason.com/blog.

Jacob Sullum, "When Booze Was Banned But Pot Was Not: What Can Today's Antiprohibitionists Learn from Their Predecessors?," *Reason*, February 2011.

Mark Thornton, "Alcohol Prohibition Was a Failure," Cato Institute Policy Report no. 157, July 17, 1991. www.cato.org.

Mark Thornton, "The Real Reason for FDR's Popularity," *Mises Daily*, October 20, 2010. www.mises.org.

Wickersham Commission Report on Alcohol Prohibition, January 7, 1931. www.druglibrary.org.

INDEX